Lotus Sutra Practice Guide

~~~~~~~~~~~~~~~~~~~~~~~~~

35-Day Practice Outline

Lotus Sutra Practice Guide: 35-Day Practice Outline

By Ryusho Jeffus

Copyright 2012 Ryusho Jeffus

Myosho-ji, Wonderful Voice Buddhist Temple
2208 Eastway Dr.
Charlotte, NC 28205

License Notes

ISBN-13: 978-1478341987
ISBN-10: 147834198X

INTRODUCTION

Frequently I am asked, how to practice, or what should a person do to practice. I am somewhat averse to giving specific instructions because I don't believe we should necessarily approach Buddhism from a strict point of view of do's and don'ts except in cases where one is in a monastery or under direction and guided personally by a teacher. Still though, Buddhism is not completely unstructured and there really needs to be some basic framework for practice.

In Nichiren Shu we have such a general frame-work which we practice in the morning and hopefully in the evening as well, which consists of reciting certain dedicatory passages, passages from the Lotus Sutra, chanting the Sacred Title, Namu Myoho Renge Kyo, and offering dedicatory prayers.

I should explain at this point something about the title of the Lotus Sutra and what Sacred Title means. The title to this Sutra can be expressed in two different ways. One way is an abbreviation, Lotus Sutra, and the other is the full or extended complete title, which is Wonderful Dharma of the Lotus Flower Sutra. The basic practice in Nichiren Buddhism is to append the two characters of Namu to the full, or what we call Sacred Title, of the Lotus Sutra. Namu comes from the Indian word Namaste, which variously translates as devotion, revere, respect, bow, honor and so forth. So when we chant the Sacred Title with Namu added we are saying that we honor the Wonderful Dharma of the Lotus Flower Sutra.

In order to understand what is going on when we do this, let me ask you to think of the title to your favorite book. Now as you think of that book, you may be aware of various images, passages, thoughts, or feelings arising within you. Depending upon how meaningful that book is those emotions may be very strong. You only need think of the title, or say the title, and many things are expressed without saying them. So too, as we chant the title to this great Sutra and as our understanding and relationship develops we connect with the contents in a very visceral way. So, chanting is kind of like an abbreviated way of saying everything that is contained within the actual Sutra itself.

As a priest and as a teacher who feels responsible to somehow make Buddhism approachable and practical to folks, especially new members I concern myself with many things. My first concern is sustainability; how to assist a new person in achieving a goal that can be sustained so the next level can be reached. My second concern is how to enable that person to learn as much of the basics, and what those basics might be, so that they can actually know what it is to be Buddhist. There are of course other considerations but those two form the basis of what I try to think about when giving initial instructions in practice.

While the optimum practice is desirable I have to worry about the ability of a person to actually follow through with such an arduous discipline when they are just beginning. It takes time to develop the skill to recite the Sutra in a meaningful and appropriate manner; time a new person may or may not be able to sustain long term. In the time in which we live folks generally expect to do things much faster and see results equally as rapidly. I don't agree with that but what I agree with has no bearing on the reality with which many people come to Buddhism.

Many people come to Buddhism because they are initially looking for some peace, some tranquility, or some joy in their lives. If they feel like a bigger burden needs to be endured to lessen other burdens they may not be willing to continue. So how do we teach people in such a way as to gently ease Buddhism into their lives, offer the chance to manifest initial benefit, which will encourage continued effort? That is the challenge.

I am generally not a fan of practicing by the clock, that is, requiring minimum time limits to practice; saying things like 'you must chant X number hours a day' or such. But when a person is just beginning I think that such a structure can have benefit. Because, if for no other reason, it gives them a stopping point, a goal, and a way to 'fit' Buddhist practice into probably an already busy schedule. In this proposal I will actually employ, as an expedient, the use of time goals.

Remember, at first bringing Buddhism to our lives is a major adjustment. There may be adjustments of space, if a sacred space is desired. There is an adjustment of thinking, if one is to pursue the philosophy. There is an adjustment of time, if one has a practice to engage in. There are many other subtle adjustments and they are not all easy to accomplish.

This book will give you an outline of daily practice, as you begin your journey along the path of the Lotus Sutra. For those who are long time practitioners of the Lotus Sutra I encourage you to actually engage in this activity as perhaps a way to reconnect yourself with your beginning practice, with the excitement and joy you had when you first began. Reconnect with your dreams, your reasons for first starting. And use this as an opportunity to refresh your practice.

My objective in this book is to accomplish the following:
1.) Basic foundation for daily practice
2.) General overview of the contents of the Lotus Sutra and basic Buddhism
3.) Learning to chant Namu Myoho Renge Kyo as a meditative practice
4.) Learn to recite portions of the Lotus Sutra
5.) Encourage a connection to Sangha
6.) Sustainable and beneficial practice for a lifetime

The only things you will need for this 35-day practice is a copy of the Lotus Sutra and this book, some pen and paper to write things down. This book is meant to be a companion guide to either the Senchu Muraon, Second Edition: 1991 or the Gene Reeves First, Edition: 2008 translation of the Lotus Sutra. You may or may not have set up a dedicated practice space in your home, either way is alright. I would suggest though if you do not have a sacred space set up at least try to practice in an unclutter area and in the same place every day. It is not necessary to have candles and incense, though you may if you wish. Statues or pictures are also not required. Eventually you may decide you wish to have some central object and for that you should approach your teacher to discuss what would be appropriate.

So, tomorrow we will begin. But first, if it not already this way, please put your copy of the Lotus Sutra on or near your altar or sacred space. This way everything you will need will be in one place and ready for you to practice uninterrupted and without distraction. Also spend the day thinking about deciding on a specific time of day you might be able to reasonably devote, for the next 35 days, to your practice. Finally write down on a piece of paper what you hope to gain from your Buddhist practice, be specific. Also think about perhaps one characteristic you would like to focus on changing over the course of this practice time. That is your practice for today. If you already are chanting then of course do so, you know you want to anyway.

~~~~~~

DAY 1

Today we begin with reading the Lotus Sutra. For the purpose of this series I will give the pages as found in the current, Second Edition: 1991, Murano (noted as M) translation. I will also provide corresponding pages from the Revees (noted as R) translation, First Edition: 2008. I will provide a beginning initial quote and then a partial ending quote. Please read from the beginning of the quote to the ending. I hope this is not too confusing. Please understand that because of copyright issues I cannot actually quote the entire passages.

I hope you can manage to get a copy of either translation. At the temple it is my policy to only quote from the Murano translation, but for this book I will offer the alternative passages from the widely available and reasonably priced Reeves version (no I do not make any commission or kickback or compensation from the sales of either or any version of the Lotus Sutra).

Ok let us begin. Today please read the following:

M p. 5 "Manjusri...Those worlds look golden-colored"
M p. 13 "Thereupon Manjusri said....the most difficult teaching in the world to believe"
R p. 56 "Manjushri....Are colored in gold"

R p. 64-65 "Then Manjushri said...That is why he displayed this omen"

Yesterday I asked you to decide on a time of day you can reasonably do this consistently every day. Today I would like for you to set a goal for the amount of time you will spend each of these days in practice. If you are new I would recommend at least 15 minutes to 25 minutes. Remember that following through with this for the entire 35 days is critical, so don't bite off more than you can chew (is that really a good expression for this endeavor).

Another thing please do this as one entire practice without interruptions. So, please do not read at one time of day and then do the practice at another time. We are trying to develop a pattern of practice here. Later on you can separate the reading from practice but for now try it this way.

I selected these passages today because while they ignore the important information concerning the size and make up of the congregation at this teaching, they do convey something important is happening. We have some pretty impressive phenomena occurring at this point and we want to know what is the reason for these things happening. Simply put, what's going on and why?

The Buddha, through these phenomena, is causing a seeking mind to develop in the congregation, this seeking mind is important to us all the time as we engage in our Buddhist practice. The Buddha wants us to ask questions.

The phenomena also herald the beginning of an important teaching, and as we read a very difficult teaching.

Now, immediately after reading this passage, I suggest that you spend the remainder of your goal time chanting Namu Myoho Renge Kyo out loud. As you chant try to clear your mind of all thoughts other than the awareness of the sound of Namu

Myoho Renge Kyo. This is a meditative practice equal to silent meditation, a practice that is as old as Buddhism and one of the foundational practices of Nichiren Buddhism. Actually, all branches of Buddhism practice this kind of vocal practice. Don't worry we won't ignore silent meditation during this 35 days, but we will focus on this key practice as specified in the Lotus Sutra.

For those who are further along in your practice and are already reciting the Sutra passages please continue to engage in this, just add the readings and the chanting instructions to your already established practice.

One note on how you should sit. If you are sitting on the floor, sit as erect as you can. Breathe in through your nose and you will exhale through your mouth as you chant. It isn't necessary to only chant one Odaimoku for each breath. The important thing is to be gentle, be rhythmical, and natural. Gently lower your eyelids till there is just a little sliver of light at the bottom. You may gaze upon the Omandala Gohonzon if you have one, though it really isn't necessary to do so. If you are sitting in a chair, please slide forward so you are sitting on the edge of your chair, this will encourage you to sit erect and not curve your spine thereby compressing your lower lungs.

As you chant if you find your mind wandering, thinking, processing, angry, resentful, tired, anxious, or anything gently bring your concentration back to Namu Myoho Renge Kyo. You may employ this little technique if it helps. Gently say to yourself the word 'thinking' and come back to your chanting.

After you have completed gradually bring yourself back to your reality, to your space. Bow and rise.

DAY 2

Read Lotus Sutra:
M p. 23 "Thereupon the World-Honored One...(page 24)...despite
these differences."
R p. 75 "At that time the World-Honored One...(page
76)...complete fundamental coherence."

Understanding by Faith

Depending upon how long it takes you to read this, and please take your time doing so, chant Namu Myoho Renge Kyo the remainder of your goal time. If your goal time is used up then just chant Namu Myoho Renge Kyo three times and bow as the conclusion of your daily practice today.

Remember; as you chant keep your mind focused on Namu Myoho Renge Kyo. It is also good while you chant to be aware of your feelings after having read this passage.

The passage we are reading today forms one of the core portions of our daily practice; chanting part of Chapter 2 and part of Chapter 16. So already you have learned an important part of Nichiren Buddhist practice.

As you read today's selection it may have seemed confusing to you, perhaps not. I would like for you, as you read to not focus too much on what the meaning is, but try to tune into what your feelings are. This may not be natural for you to do, but give it a try.

In this daily practice outline we won't be going through every detail of the Lotus Sutra there will be some important doctrinal points not covered. It isn't my intent to make this a thorough doctrinal exploration of the Lotus Sutra; that isn't possible in 35 days. Instead, my goal is to connect you with a spirit or feeling of the richness of the Lotus Sutra as an important Buddhist text.

In today's reading this point actually is brought up. The Lotus Sutra, what the Buddha is teaching, is very difficult to understand, and the Buddha is telling one of his disciples just this point. Over and over in the Lotus Sutra the Buddha says that our connection with the Lotus Sutra occurs not on the level of the mind or intellect but on the level of heart or belief.

The Lotus Sutra comes to much of the Western world in a somewhat disguised way. By that I mean it has come to us outside the context in which it occurs in much of the East Asian countries. In the long history of Buddhism virtually all Buddhists have considered the Lotus Sutra a very important text, we don't see that so much now in the West. We tend to see the Lotus Sutra outside its relationship to other texts and other denominations. It is almost as if the Lotus Sutra is orphaned from its own history.

I don't believe I have it in my capacity to really convey the richness and importance of the Lotus Sutra, certainly not in this short 35 days. I will try though, to connect you with some of the spirit, grandeur, richness, and great joy expressed in this wonderful if not confusing teaching. To that end, I encourage you to be confused by the confusing, be awed by the spectacular, and be joyful at the promise of enlightenment. Read with me, read with your heart.

Today the Buddha says that, since he began he has been teaching the Dharma through various methods trying to convey the wisdom of Buddhas. This wisdom is very hard to

14

understand. It is complex and confusing, partly because the Buddhas try to teach so many different people with different abilities. In this section the Buddha makes the statement that in spite of all that has been heard to this point, it still doesn't represent the hidden core of Buddhism.

During Nichiren's time and before, the great teachers of Buddhism recognized that the Lotus Sutra was an important text, but they also said because it is difficult to understand they would not teach it. Nichiren, however, countered that because it represents the heart of the Buddha's teachings, and because the Buddha recognized its difficult and complex nature yet still said it should be taught in the future it was most appropriate to teach it now. So in brief, it is hard to understand yet that is no reason not to follow it in this time.

DAY 3

Read Lotus Sutra:
M p. 36 "Any Saravaka or Bodhisattva....(p. 37)...Exactly as I am."
R p. 88 "If a sharavaka or a bodhisattva...(p. 89)...Without any distinctions."

Becoming a Buddha

Again, today complete the remainder of your goal time chanting Namu Myoho Renge Kyo. Remember as you chant keep your mind focused on the chanting, this is a meditative practice. If you find your mind wandering say the word 'thinking' to yourself and gently come back to your chanting.

I selected today's reading because of the great promise contained within it. You will become a Buddha just by your exposure to this powerful heart of all the Dharma!

There are not a large variety of teachings of Buddhism, from the perspective of the Lotus Sutra, except as expedients for this single purpose of all Buddhas; to enable everyone to become enlightened.

It sounds amazing doesn't it? Perhaps you are skeptical, that is perfectly natural, so were the Buddha's contemporary disciples. Some of his disciples actually left when they heard this. In the part preceding this section some five hundred actually got up and left choosing to ignore this great promise. We also have this choice to make as we practice the Lotus Sutra. We can choose to continue and try or we can say to heck with it and abandon the practice.

The interesting thing here is that there is no punishment for abandoning this teaching. It isn't like you will be punished or receive retribution; Buddhism doesn't operate that way, unlike other religions. Simply put, walking away only delays the eventual awakening. The Lotus Sutra, according to the Buddha is the heart and soul of all of Buddhism, even if it is difficult. Because it is at the core of Buddhism it is a truth that will eventually manifest in a person's life, even if in a future lifetime.

For those of you who are eager and think this is going to slowly, check your patience. This undertaking is only 3 days old and we are not in a hurry, this is a lifetime endeavor so go slowly and savor each of these steps. Enjoy! Have a great day today, and if you want to go ahead and do more then consider chanting during some activity you are engaged in today, but we will talk more about this later. Also keep in mind we are trying to engage in an activity that is both consistent and rhythmical. We also are trying to practice with the long term in mind, keeping it going over the long haul of a lifetime.

DAY 4

Read Lotus Sutra:
M p.48 "The Bodhisattvas who hear the Dharma...(to end of chapter)".
R p.100 "When bodhisattvas hear this Dharma...(to end of chapter)".

"When you have great joy you will become Buddhas!"
(Lotus Sutra, Chapter II)

For those who have read my writings for a while you know that this passage is one I frequently quote. I think it is key and provides us with a hint as to how to practice. If we can begin to generate a spark of joy in our lives as we chant and practice the Lotus Sutra, it is my belief that this will eventually spread throughout our lives and become a foundation for how we can live.

We may be weighted down by all manner of burdens in our lives. Yet, I do feel that when we chant and read the Lotus Sutra, if for even a moment we can suspend our dwelling on those burdens and experience a small amount of joy in our lives because of our relationship to and practice of the Lotus Sutra. It can be the foundation for a shift in our lives that will have far reaching impact on all of our sufferings. Is it easy in ways, yet because it is easy it can be difficult to accomplish!

It does require a loosening of the tight grasp we have on our sufferings. When we dwell on our sufferings it can create a sense of security, we feel pain so we know we are alive. I think we become accustomed to living this way without even realizing it. We lament our lives which seems to create a sense

19

of being alive and we become fearful of letting it all go and not being attached to those things.

I had it in my notes to give some basic instructions about chanting at the beginning of this series, but for some reason I failed to write them. Today according to my outline I would like for you to do some silent meditation. I'll give some basic instructions, which I hope you will use both during silent meditation as well as chanting meditation. Of course this is not the only way to meditate, but it is a basic method that I can share with you in this book. If you know other ways of meditation that is fine, however for this practice I encourage you to try this. If it just doesn't work for you then by all means go with what is most helpful.

Also as you read the sutra passages, try to be in touch with how you feel after reading. Perhaps you feel confused, that is fine, it is good that you identify this. Perhaps you feel excitement, or joy, or even sorrow. All of those are perfectly acceptable. Focus on your feelings without trying to understand the meaning so much. Be gentle on yourself.

Today let's do some silent meditation. Begin by chanting Namu Myoho Renge Kyo three times. Then get in a comfortable sitting position. This sitting position should be erect opening up your lower abdomen area as much as possible. Try not to slouch as this closes off your ability to breathe deeply and comfortably. As you sit in a mediation posture, sit erect, eyes partially closed, legs crossed if sitting on the floor or sitting forward on a chair with feet flat on the floor legs uncrossed. Hold your hands, left over right palm, palm up just above your belly button, the center of your life energy. Begin by breathing in through your nose and then slowly exhaling from between your lips. As you slowly exhale concentrate you mind on Namu Myoho Renge Kyo. As you exhale slowly also chant very slowly in your mind drawing out the Namu Myoho Renge Kyo for the entire breath. Breathe in through your nose and exhale from between your lips. Do this for 5 Minutes to 7 minutes max. If you find your mind wandering just say to yourself a simple word such as 'thinking' and come back to the out breath and Namu Myoho Renge Kyo.

When your time has elapsed chant Namu Myoho Renge Kyo three times out loud slowly, bow and finish.

DAY 5

(See Appendix One for Shidoku of Chapter 16)

Today we begin to tackle the reading of Chapter 16 in Shindoku. You will find a Romanized text the portion of Chapter 16 which is read during services in Nichiren Shu in the Appendix of this book. This important portion of the Lotus Sutra is read in all denominations of Nichiren Buddhism.

Let me explain a little about Shindoku so you will have an idea of what it is. Shindoku could be considered a liturgical language. Though it wasn't originally considered as such in this modern time, it has taken on the aspect of such. By liturgical language I mean it is a special language that really isn't spoken by anyone as a matter of course. It is kind of like the position of Latin today. It really isn't a living language, and many people who might otherwise be familiar with it do not actually know what it means without special training.

The pronunciation of Shindoku is based upon the Chinese characters, which I have omitted for ease of reading. I will note here that the omission of the Chinese characters is not considered the best thing to do and is discouraged normally. I am however breaking with this convention in this instance simply as an expedient to make the reading easier, perhaps or hopefully so.

Back to Shindoku, as I mentioned it is a Japanese reading of the Chinese characters that has its origins way back to the 8th century or so when Chinese writing and culture was brought to Japan. Without going into a lot of detail you could say it is archaic. It is not easily recognizable to either the Chinese or to the Japanese when spoken, though it is readable if one is trained, and more easily read by Chinese.

There is some debate as to whether or not we need to continue the practice of reading in Shindoku as non Japanese or non Chinese. Some people say it isn't necessary and we shouldn't emphasize the practice, others disagree. I myself fall on the side of continuing the practice of using Shindoku and do so at the temple for all of our services.

My reason for doing this is to assist in creating a transcendent experience as we do our Sutra practice. It may not have been the original intent when Shindoku reading was begun, but it wasn't too long after it started when it was not easily intelligible to most people. When we read this section in our native language I feel there is too much of a tendency to focus on the meanings of the words. While knowing what it says is important, since this is the most important part of the Lotus Sutra, I feel that when doing service it is potentially more beneficial to open ourselves up to a transcendent experience. This is just my opinion, and so it may not be more valuable than other differing opinions.

Today for your practice, especially if you are new to the practice, I would like for you to begin to try to read the Shindoku of Chapter 16 in the Appendix. This may be slow and very tedious. Please do not try to read the entire portion, I don't want you to become frustrated. I do not know of anyone, who when they began, could easily get through the entire thing, even Japanese people struggle.

Today just read as much as you are able to read in your goal time minus 5 minutes. Leave 5 minutes to yourself to chant Namu Myoho Renge Kyo. Be at peace with however much of the chapter you are able to read. Later on we will be reading the English so for right now just open yourself up to the mystery of the passage.

A short note on pronunciation standards. For those familiar with Spanish vowels they are the exact same. In English there is a slight difference. 'A' is pronounced as a short 'a' sound like 'ah'. 'I' is pronounced as a long 'e' sound like 'ee'. 'U' is pronounced like 'oo' in hoot. 'E' is pronounced like a long 'a' sound as in eh. 'O' is pronounced like a long 'o' sound as in row. 'EI' is pronounced like the long 'a' sound in hay. 'AI' is pronounced like the long 'i' sound in I. This is a rough guide to get you started.

The key today is to just get started doing this important practice. Again, this is a meditative practice, so to the extent you are able keep, your mind focused on the sounds. Be tuned in to all of your feelings, they are neither good nor bad, they just are.

DAY 6

Read Lotus Sutra
M p. 61 first paragraph "Sariputra! Suppose there lived.....(end
of second paragraph p. 63).....the large cars of treasures?"
R p. 112 last paragraph "Shariputra, suppose in a village....(end
of last paragraph p. 114)....guilty of falsehood or not?"

Parable of the Burning House

Today we read the most widely known and most popular parable found in the Lotus Sutra. This parable is probably the most widely cited section of the Lotus Sutra, even by people who are unfamiliar with or who do not espouse the importance of the Lotus Sutra.

Today is a long read, but it is a good one. As I mentioned in the beginning of this series I wanted to introduce you to some of the grandeur and richness of the Lotus Sutra. This is one of those moments in the Lotus Sutra where this is revealed.

Once you have read this portion spend the rest of your time chanting. Again, as you chant try to keep your mind focused on the actual pronunciation of Namu Myoho Renge Kyo, if you find your mind wandering gently bring it back to your chanting by saying to yourself 'thinking'.

There are many things to consider once you have read this portion of chapter 3. I have only highlighted one small portion, and after you finish your practice today perhaps if you have some time you might find it interesting to read more, but don't let extra reading take away from your actual practice time.

The story of the Burning House is really about our practice of Buddhism. We are constantly living in a burning house, a house of the sufferings of life. Sometimes we distract ourselves from these sufferings by indulging in a variety of things, all basically misguided attempts to eliminate suffering but actually often contributing to more suffering.

Buddhism presents us with a way to enjoy life, to eliminate suffering, and to contribute to not only our own well being but also the well being of our entire environment, including other people around us. The Buddha offered a wide variety of teachings prior to the Lotus Sutra and in the Lotus Sutra he explains why there were so many different teachings. They served as a means to enable people to partake of the ultimate purpose of all Buddhas, that is enlightenment.

This is represented in the variety of carts offered to the children to entice them to leave the burning house. When the children emerge they are rewarded not with the smaller carts they initially sought but with grander carts, equaling the enlightenment of all Buddhas.

I hope you have enjoyed your practice to this point. Please rest assured that you are making good progress towards your emancipation from sufferings. The process is slow but it is methodical, just don't become impatient or discouraged. During these first few days, it is my intent that you begin to easily incorporate Buddhist practice into your life. The fact that you are doing so is a fundamental part of preparing for a lifelong journey.

If you think about those smooth river rocks people seem to like so much, or if you consider the Grand Canyon, small but continuous erosions made those things possible. So too with your own life, you are slowly making changes that will have lasting and beautiful impact on your life.

DAY 7

Read Lotus Sutra
M p. 76 "Sariputra! With this
parable I expounded.....(top of p.
80).....The stage of avaivartika."
R p. 127 "Shariputra, it is for the
sake of all beings....(top of p.
131)...."Will never backslide."

Buddhist Fundamentals

Today we continue reading a bit more of Chapter III. Today's reading presents me with a bit of a difficulty. This one section to me highlights the most important complaint I have for the Reeves translation. In the Reeves translation not once is what has come to be known as the Eightfold Path mentioned yet in the Murano it is mentioned twice. If we examine other translations we also see this mentioning of "eight right ways".

One of the points frequently mentioned as I teach the Lotus Sutra is that within the Lotus Sutra is contained all of the important previous teachings of the Buddha. The Lotus Sutra is not an abandoning of previous teachings it is in stead, an advancement on or beyond those previous teachings. All of the Buddhas teachings are still important and necessary and are contained in the Lotus Sutra.

In this section we read about the Four Noble Truths as well as the mentioning of the importance of the Eightfold Path or Eight Right Ways.

29

For those new to Buddhism I'll offer a short introduction to these two teachings. There is much on the web available that will expand on this brief introduction to perhaps the two most fundamental teachings of the Buddha.

The Four Noble Truths was the first teaching of the Buddha after he attained enlightenment and presents the foundation or cornerstone for all of Buddhism.

The Four Noble Truths are in brief:
1) The truth of suffering
2) The truth of the origin of suffering
3) The truth of the cessation of suffering
4) The truth of the path leading to the cessation of suffering.

The **Eightfold Path**, the path leading to the cessation of suffering is:
1) Right View
2) Right Intention
3) Right Speech
4) Right Action
5) Right Livelihood
6) Right effort
7) Right Mindfulness
8) Right Concentration.

Let me point out here that 'right' in the above is not the opposite of 'wrong'. Right in the above is about doing those things which will yield the greatest good. In Buddhism it is not merely enough to do no harm, we are striving to do the greatest good. We call this living skillfully, and that is what we strive to do when following these Eight Right Ways.

Not all of the time will we be presented with clear choices, sometimes our options may all be less than favorable. In all things though our intention, our basis for action, is to do the least harm and the greatest good.

I encourage you to look up deeper explanations of the above concepts. You can find some on my blog as well as various places on the Internet.

From today, as a new practitioner of Buddhism you have a guideline for living your daily life. You may have noticed that up until today we just focused on cultivating a daily practice routine. From today though you know a little bit more about what being a Buddhist means in the context of your daily life.

Congratulations on your seventh day of practice and to the beginning of your walk on the path to enlightenment!

DAY 8

Read Lotus Sutra
M p.89 "World-Honored One! Allow....(p. 92)...It has come to me
unexpectedly."
R p. 142 "World-Honored One, we would...(p. 144)....have now
come to me by themselves."

Parable of the Rich Man and His Poor Son

Today is long read, none-the-less, try to read all of it within
your goal time and what ever time you have remaining spend it
chanting Namu Myoho Renge Kyo. As you chant do so with
great joy, even a small amount of joy is the cause for even
greater joy. Think of the great treasure you have come into
contact with because of your practice of Buddhism and the
Lotus Sutra.

Yesterday you learned of the Eightfold Path. Beginning today
for the next 7 days try to focus on one of those eight right ways.
Make this the focus of your practice outside of your dedicated
time reading and chanting. You might pick Right Speech and
then for the rest of the week try, to the best of your ability, to
only engage in speech that, not only causes no harm, but
encourages good. Or you might pick another of the Eight Right
Things. Focus on one, maybe even write it on a card and tape it
to your computer or bathroom mirror to remind you of your
intention.

Actually this kind of setting your intention is engaging in
another of the Eight Right Ways, that of Right Intention. See
how easy it is to do this practice, or at least try to do the

practice. If in the course of this week you should mess up or forget, please do not worry about it. Use it as a lesson to advance your growth.

This parable of the rich man and his poor son is often mistakenly compared to the prodigal son in the Bible. It should be noted though that the two stories are different in many key ways. In this story the son has left his father at an early age before his father had any wealth. The son had no knowledge of the great treasure he was entitled too. The son in this story did not avoid doing the hard work it took to elevate his life.

We are like the poor son and the Buddha is like the rich father. We may feel no connection, or we may feel that we are not deserving of great joy. We may be just like the son who runs in fear of the man who is his father. We may run from the promise of enlightenment, thinking we are not worthy or that it isn't possible for us to be happy.

Yet, through your daily practice of Buddhism you can slowly elevate your life condition and see potentials for unimaginable benefits.

Never fear, there is no such person who is not capable or deserving of attaining enlightenment. If Anguli Mala, or Devedatta can attain enlightenment then there is nothing that can stand in the way of our own enlightenment, if we only try.

If you have not done so already, I encourage you to write on a card one thing you would like to change over this 35-day practice period. Put this card in your sacred space if you have one, let it be a reminder of what has brought you to this Buddhist practice. If you are the kind of person who writes a journal perhaps each day you can reflect on your goal.

You are beginning your second week of practice. This is great; keep focused on your daily efforts.

DAY 9

*Read Lotus Sutra
M p. 105 from beginning of Chapter
V to p. 106 end of first full
paragraph
R p. 159 from beginning of Chapter
V to p. 160 end of third full
paragraph*

Simile of Herbs

This is one of several short similes and parables found in the Lotus Sutra. Today after you finish reading this short section spend half your remaining time practicing to read the Shindoku portion of Chapter 16. We will continually come back to this so that you can gain greater skill at saying this important portion of the Lotus Sutra. The other half of your practice time spend chanting Namu Myoho Renge Kyo.

Yesterday I suggested that you pick out one of the Eightfold Path or Eight Right Ways to focus on during the course of your day. I hope you will continue to focus on this same Right Way for the entire week. I think sometimes it is easier to really focus on one thing at first and perhaps achieve some success rather than try to remember all eight, get confused and overwhelmed, and become discouraged. Remember we are taking this one day at a time preparing for a lifetime endeavor.

35

This short story we read today is important for a variety of reasons. One thing this short story demonstrates is that the Buddha's teaching is equally available to everyone and we each absorb it and manifest it according to our unique capacities. No matter what our capabilities or capacities are the rain of the Dharma provides nourishment to all with out distinction.

The rain of the Dharma nourishes all the plants even though some are tall and some are not, some are fruit trees, some are flowering bushes, the distinctions are endless but the Dharma is universal and not dependent upon the capacity or capability of the one receiving the nourishment.

Though it is not in the short portion I suggested reading today it does appear in this chapter the merit or the promise of what we should expect because of our practice of Buddhism and the Lotus Sutra. The promise is of being peaceful in our present lives, nothing material, this is not a prosperity practice, this is about being peaceful and at ease. There is no basis or proof that material prosperity either induces or directly influences being peaceful and at ease.

Again, today after reading the short section from the sutra, split your remaining time between practicing the reading of Chapter 16 in Shindoku and chanting Namu Myoho Renge Kyo. Also continue focusing on one of the Eight Right things without becoming discouraged if you forget or are unable to fully do it. Intention is key!

DAY 10

Read Lotus Sutra
M p. 117 "Great Hero, World-Honored One!...(continue to p.
118)....Like the man who was permitted to take the meal."
R p. 171 "Great Hero, World-Honored one,....(continue to p.
172)...As you would tell a starving person to eat!"

Starving Man

After you have finished reading this short section from
Chapter VI divide the remainder of your goal time between
reading the Shindoku of Chapter 16 and chanting Odaimoku.

Chapter VI is the first of several specific predictions of future
enlightenment given to various people in the congregation at
the preaching of the Lotus Sutra. These various predictions are
meant to show that enlightenment is attainable by anyone.
This is a pretty awesome promise and one that may seem
unbelievable. And this sentiment is brought out in the passage
we read today.

The speakers, since this is actually said by several people in
unison, tell the Buddha that even though they heard it from
him, that they would become enlightened they still had doubts,
and even fears that perhaps this prediction does not apply to
them.

I gave a lecture on the many predictions of future
enlightenment in which I talk about how these serve to
provide, both those receiving the predictions as well as all who
read the Lotus Sutra with hope. In the study of hope theory
there are several key components that serve to engender hope

in an individual. Two of those are community and a future story.

When we come to practice Buddhism we all come from a variety of places, physically, spiritually, and emotionally. We join together with others who are at once similar and also very different than ourselves. We practice together in concert with these people and we see the powerful effects of Buddhism on their lives. This is fertile ground for the development of a future story that can be markedly different from what we are currently experiencing.

These predictions of future enlightenment are a story of a future of joy, of the cessation of suffering, peace, and enlightenment for ourselves. What the Buddha is encouraging us to do is to rethink our image of what we perceive our future to be. No longer do we need to suffer, no longer do we need to be insecure, no longer do we need to wonder if happiness will ever come to us.

Today as you continue to read the Lotus Sutra, and chant Namu Myoho Renge Kyo, and of course continue observing your selected Right Way, also think about what your future would be like if you overcame the sufferings you may currently be dealing with. You should know that no matter what point you start from on the path to enlightenment, no matter what your past has been, no matter what you think you are capable of, enlightenment is not just a possibility but a certainty if you continue your practice. If even the worst of the worst, as I have mentioned before, can attain enlightenment through the practice of Buddhism then you certainly can as well.

Do not be as the starving man and fear to partake of this wonderful Dharma. Take this Dharma, practice and partake of the nourishment of the Buddha's teachings. Do not fear that you don't know what to do, have faith in the Lotus Sutra, and continue chanting Namu Myoho Renge Kyo.

DAY 11

Read Lotus Sutra
M p. 129 "In order to save all living beings....(continue to p. 130)....The Most Honorable One."
M p. 140 "Then he expounded the teaching.....(read entire paragraph).....suffering and lamentation are eliminated."
R p. 182 "In order to liberate living beings,....(read to p. 183)....To one of unexcelled honor."
R p. 194 "Then he taught the twelve causes and conditions....(read entire paragraph)...suffering and anguish are extinguished."

12 Link Chain of Causation

After reading these sections spend the remainder of your practice time chanting Namu Myoho Renge Kyo. At the end of today's writing I'll have another activity for you to engage in.

In the first section of today's read we hear of the praise being offered to the Buddha. I think it is important to look closely at the praise, not because it talks about the great things the Buddha accomplished for himself, but for the benefit he provided all humanity.

If the Buddha had attained enlightenment and kept it for himself we would not even be practicing Buddhism today. I personally am also of the mind that if the Buddha had not shared his great accomplishment with others, then his own personal enlightenment would have vanished just as dew evaporates with the rising sun.

Why do I say this? It is because at the heart of Buddhism are our connections, our relationships with all of life. We do not exist in a vacuum, and so our own personal enlightenment resides within the context of the happiness of others. Just as the Buddha is the leader of all mankind in the quest for the elimination of suffering, so too are we leaders in our own individual ways, providing an example of the possibilities.

Today we are presented yet again in the Lotus Sutra to one of the Buddha's major teachings. This Twelve Link Chain is a way of looking at the cause and effect relationship within our lives. The Buddha taught that the key to breaking the chain of rebirth was to eliminate ignorance and he set out to free us from this bond.

The Twelve Link Chain also indirectly points to the reality that nothing arises independent of some cause and relationship. If we examine our lives closely we can see our myriad connections to countless others, because of these connections we are able to live our lives. Our very own existence is only possible because of the countless efforts of many others, beginning with our own parents who gave birth to us and who provided us with food and care at birth, a time when we were most helpless.

As we continue to live our lives we sometimes loose sight of these connections and think of ourselves as independent beings. Because of this thinking we are sometimes led to believe that we do not need other people, or we don't need some people, and yet the truth is that even as we grow older and live seemingly independent lives we are still tied to the efforts, the labors of countless others.

Today please continue with observing the one Right Way you have chosen to follow this week. Do not be discouraged if at times you forget, it is natural at times to get caught up in the events of our lives and not be mindful. Remember this is practice and as practice we continue to try our best.

Also today when you sit down to eat your meal, no matter where you are, try to think about the many people who have made the meal possible. See if you can engage in this activity while you eat slowly. Let appreciation well up from within you as your taste buds are activated. Think of the people who built your car with all of its complex components that work together to provide transportation. Or think of the bus driver or train engineers. Think of those who laid the roads or rails. Think of the cashier who stands on their feet all day long ringing up purchases. Think of the truck driver who delivered the merchandise to the store. Think of the packagers. Think of the farm laborers who make the food possible. Think of those in oil producing countries who provide their natural resources and labor. The list is almost endless. I can imagine that by the end of the meal you still have not thought of all the countless labors, big and small, that made that meal possible. Don't forget to include your own labors as well.

DAY 12

Read Lotus Sutra
M p. 144 "I will tell you a parable....(continue to p. 145)....I divide the One Vehicle of the Buddha into three only expediently."
R p. 198 "Suppose there was a bad road.....(continue to p. 199)....made distinctions within it, and spoken of the three."

Parable of A Magic City

After you have completed reading this short section from the Lotus Sutra spend the balance of your time split between reciting as much of Chapter 16 as you are able and chanting Namu Myoho Renge Kyo. I hope that you are still trying to follow this model to the best of your ability. Remember we are trying to establish a daily practice regimen of both practice and study.

Eventually I hope that you will expand your time so that you can have more for study and more for practice, however at this point it is important to try to be as consistent as possible, that is what is important now. We want to remember the image of the water flowing constantly, and through this constant gradual action slowly polishing the rocks.

Today we read another of the famous and major parables found in the Lotus Sutra. This parable tells of a group of travelers who have heard of a fantastic city to which they wish to travel. The road to this city is dangerous and they do not have the skill necessary to get there on their own. They learn of a skilled guide who can take them and so they contact him to do so. Along the way the group becomes tired and discouraged and even wishes to return home.

Seeing that the group is becoming discouraged the guide conjures up a magic city where the people take rest and nourishment. Once the group is refreshed the guide tells them, that where they are is not the real final destination, it is just so they can become refreshed. So the group then sets out for the final destination.

This story is given so that people will understand why all of the different teachings of Buddhism exist. They exist solely for the purpose, according to the Lotus Sutra, of preparing or leading to the one great truth presented within the Lotus Sutra, that of enlightenment of all living beings equal to that of the Buddha. Buddhas teach the various other teachings, much the same way the guide conjured up the magic city, as a way to encourage practitioners along the path to enlightenment.

If the Buddha had revealed his ultimate purpose early on people would have been discouraged thinking it too difficult. So then you might be wondering well what is different about people now and people then? Why are we given and encouraged to practice the Lotus Sutra first? Why is it taught in the Lotus Sutra that this sutra should be the single most important sutra in the age in which we live?

My feeling on this is because in this age the Buddha suspected that there would be an abundance of variations on his original teachings, that this abundance would present confusing choices for people of later ages. We see this hinted at in various portions of the Lotus Sutra when he talks about an age where there are many false teachings and false teachers.

Contained within the Lotus Sutra are all of the Buddha's previous teachings, according to the studies of Nichiren this sutra represents not just the culmination of the purpose of the

Buddha it also represents the complete teachings of the Buddha. There is nothing more and there is nothing missing in this one single teaching and no other teaching offers this. Therefore to have protected and transmitted this single sutra through the ages became important, and continues to be so, because of this completeness. I don't believe it is so much that this is the only way to practice Buddhism, but that this way, this practicing the Lotus Sutra, is the most complete way and offers the way by which anyone can attain enlightenment equal to that of the Buddha.

Remember to continue working on the one Right Way you selected at the beginning of this second week of your practice. Also continue when possible to keep thinking of your connections to people as you engage in different activities throughout your day.

DAY 13

*Read Lotus Sutra
M p. 153 First two paragraphs of
Chapter VIII
M p. 156 "My disciples are
performing...The listeners will
doubt me."
M p. 161 "World-Honored One!
Suppose a man visited....(to the end
of the paragraph)...You will not be
short of anything you want."
R p. 207 First two paragraphs of
Chapter VIII
R p. 210 "Using innumerable skillful
means....Would be doubtful and perplexed."
R p. 215 "World-Honored One, it is as if....(read two
paragraphs)....and be free from all poverty and want."*

Parable of the Gem in the Robe

Today's reading consists of three short sections found in
Chapter VIII. As in the previous days split your time between
reciting Chapter 16 in Shindoku and chanting Namu Myoho
Renge Kyo. Keep in mind consistency and steady effort.

I presented three short reading today because I wanted to have
you read first of the great joy experienced by one of the
Buddha's major disciples, Purna. In the first paragraph we
hear of the joy of Purna because of these great things;
assurance of future enlightenment of the great disciples of the
Buddha, hearing of the previous lives of the Buddha, hearing

the great powers of the Buddha. Having heard these three great things, things never before revealed, the disciple Purna expresses both his joy and his admiration.

I should mention a little about Purna. He was, as I mentioned, one of the Buddhas major disciples, one of the 10 listed as the most important. Purna is noteworthy because of his great efforts to spread the teachings of the Buddha. The Buddha says "I always praise him, saying that he is the most excellent expounder of the Dharma." Purna, after the death of the Buddha was largely responsible for the spread of Buddhism in what is now Southeast Asia. The icon representing Purna is the egoro, or hand held incense burner.

When I began this temple in Charlotte I selected Purna as the person and spirit I wanted to model and in fact an egoro decorates one of the Sutra boxes in the main hall, hondo.

The next section you read talks about the many forms the disciples of the Buddha take on as they engage in Buddhist practice. It also talks about how sometimes these forms exhibit what would be considered not so skillful attributes by pretending to have the three poisons of greed, anger, and ignorance. In a way we might consider this to represent the many different kinds of people who will practice Buddhism in this age.

Finally in the selections today we also read of another of the famous or important parables found in the Lotus Sutra. See, I told you this sutra was full of interesting stories.

The parable of the gem in the robe is very short, only one paragraph long in the Murano translation. Yet in spite of its brevity it packs a very powerful message.

In each of us is already the enlightened nature or potential. Enlightenment isn't something we have to bring into our lives, it is already resident. The practice of Buddhism isn't so much about becoming someone different, as it is about becoming who we really are. We do not take on enlightenment from outside ourselves, but develop what we already have. We have the gem, we just need to take it out and use it, there is no need for us to continue our sufferings.

DAY 14

Read Lotus Sutra
M p. 164 first two paragraphs Chapter IX
M p. 166 single paragraph "Good men! Ananda and I
resolved....assured of his future Buddhahood."
M p. 167 single paragraph "In your future life.....just as you are
now mine."
R p. 219 first paragraph Chapter IX
R p. 221 single paragraph "The World-Honored One,...So now he
receives this assurance."
R p. 221 last paragraph "Then the Buddha spoke to Rahula..." to
end of paragraph on page 222

Ananda and Rahula

Congratulations! Today is the last day of your second week of practicing Nichiren Buddhism. You have come a long way; I hope you can celebrate this achievement.

After you finish reading the above passages I hope you will spend the balance of your practice time chanting Namu Myoho Renge Kyo with great joy and fulfillment. Remember as you chant to keep your mind focused on the chanting as much as you are able. If you find your mind straying remember to say something like 'thinking' to yourself and come back to the chanting.

Today we are formally introduced to Ananda, though he has been with us since we began reading the Lotus Sutra. Ananda, one of the Buddha's 10 most important disciples was foremost in knowing the teachings of the Buddha and it is said that he was always with the Buddha whenever the Buddha taught. It is because of Ananda's great memory and his devotion to the Buddha that we have the teachings of the Buddha today.

At the first Buddhist Counsel it was Ananda who recited from memory all that the Buddha taught. At the Beginning of Sutras appears the phrase "Thus have I heard" which indicates that the Sutra is being recounted or retold by Ananda. At the First Buddhist Counsel Ananda would recount the teachings and all the others would then commit them to their memory as well, and so began the collecting and preserving of the teachings of the Buddha.

Rahula was the Buddha's son who also became an important disciple of Buddhism and the Buddha. It is the section concerning Rahula's future enlightenment that I would like to spend a little time with. As we read this paragraph we see the many titles that will be attributed to the Buddha he will become.

But notice that Rahula really does no specific noteworthy thing except make offerings to Buddha's. He is the eldest son of those Buddhas just as he is now. Unlike many others noted in the Lotus Sutra who perform specific practices and accomplish various achievements Rahula does not. This is considered to be a Secret Practice or a practice as nobody special but a person who practices strenuously and thereby leads others to faith through friendship.

For many of us this is where the heart of our practice lies. We are not noteworthy people; most of us are rather ordinary, living ordinary and mundane lives. Yet it is by carrying out our Buddhist practice in such a simple way that we are able to lead countless people we interact with daily to Buddhism. When we become happy, when we change our lives, as ordinary people, others around us who also are leading simple lives can be moved to praise Buddhism, which is the first step to faith.

As the son of the Buddha I imagine Rahula lived with a lot of stress and pressure and yet always in the shadow of his teacher, his father. It is not an easy place to practice. If we think of the Buddha's cousin, Devedatta we see that he succumbed to jealousy and even envy of the Buddha and sought to kill the Buddha. Rahula on the other hand lived quietly and meekly never causing problems and never seeking fame based upon his relationship to his father.

Being content with ourselves as we awaken to the Buddha residing in our lives is not easy. We may think that we are not doing enough for Buddhism, but we should never feel this way. It is the ordinariness of our lives and our ability to attain enlightenment that will be most encouraging to others.

DAY 15

Read Lotus Sutra
M p. 171 "If after my extinction anyone rejoices...(continue to p. 173 end of first paragraph)...be able to attain Anuttara-samyak-sambodhi."
R p. 225 "Again addressing Medicine King,...(continue to p. 227 end of first paragraph)...they attain supreme awakening."

Five Practices

After you finish reading this section of the Lotus Sutra spend the remainder of your practice time chanting Namu Myoho Renge Kyo. Congratulations, you are beginning your third week of practicing and studying the Lotus Sutra. This is noteworthy!

You may have noticed as you read the Sutra today that a change has taken place here. One thing, now we see exactly how we are supposed to practice the Lotus Sutra, and another is a shift in tense from those present to those who will come after the death of the Buddha.

I heard once that there is a belief that this chapter, Chapter X is perhaps the oldest part of the Lotus Sutra. I don't know for certain the truth of this statement but we can see the emergence of ideas that appear in other chapters begin in this chapter.

The five practices of the Lotus Sutra are; to keep, to read, to recite, to expound, and to copy.

By keep it is meant that we try to observe all the teachings found in the Lotus Sutra, we try to hold them in our heart and manifest them in our lives. Last week I asked you to focus on trying to practice one of the Eight Right Ways. I wonder how you did? Were you able to make any changes in the way you live based on trying to follow the one you selected? I hope you had some success, remember even a little success is better than nothing. This week, continue to try to observe the Right Way you selected and then add one more to your efforts this week. So now you will begin focusing on observing or keeping Two of the Eight Right Ways.

To read means to do exactly as you have been doing these past two weeks. Reading is different than reciting in that one is from a study perspective and the other is from a ritual perspective, that is one way of looking at it. Every day I have suggested short sections for you to read over and think about. As you can see there is much more that we have not read, but you can come back to that gradually after you finish the 35 days of practice here.

To recite, as I mentioned above is more of a ritual formal practice. Reciting is doing things like reading the Shindoku of Chapter 16 you have been working on mastering. Recite, in the context of our formal service also includes reciting a portion of Chapter II, which I had you read early on in this activity. Recite also includes the chanting of Namu Myoho Renge Kyo, which is the Sacred Title of the Lotus Sutra. We believe, as Nichiren taught, that by reciting Namu Myoho Renge Kyo we are in fact reciting the entirety of the Lotus Sutra. If you think of your favorite book, and some one mentions the title to that book, many images, thoughts, memories, emotions can occur in your mind just by saying the title of your favorite book. So too with

56

Namu Myoho Renge Kyo, especially as we learn more about what is contained within the Lotus Sutra.

To expound means to teach or to tell others of the great truths found in the Lotus Sutra, as well as to share the joys you experience as a result of your ongoing practice. It is important to understand that it isn't necessary to be a scholar in order to share what you have learned and experienced through your practice, all you need is your sincere heart. There is a story of one of the Buddha's disciples who had only met the Buddha a few short days before. While traveling on a road he came upon a stranger to whom he extolled the greatness and joy of Buddhism. The man asked him to explain more and the disciple said he had only met the Buddha but he would take the man to see the Buddha. The man accepted the offer but declared that he would take faith in Buddhism based upon the disciple's sincere heart.

To copy means to actually write out the Lotus Sutra. In Nichiren Shu we actually have a meditative practice called Shakyo, which means to write out the Lotus Sutra.

Finally, let me close today by pointing out, as I mentioned earlier, that in this section we read we are now looking forward into the future to a time after the Buddha has died. We see the great promise of enlightenment given to those who practice and have faith in the Lotus Sutra at this time. We see that they, meaning us, will be born in an evil world, a world where Buddhist ideals are not widely observed. We see that the people who appear after the Buddha's life and practice the Lotus Sutra actually have given up rewards of good karma just so they can practice in this time and lead countless people to faith in the Lotus Sutra.

We are doing the work of the Buddha; we are the Buddha's messengers. The Buddha even says that a person who speaks ill of the Buddha in his presence is not as bad as a person who speaks ill of people who practice in the ages after the Buddha has died. We can see by this that the Buddha places special great importance on the people who appear after the Buddha and maintain faith in the Lotus Sutra.

Congratulations again to you!

DAY 16

Read Lotus Sutra
M p. 175 "I have expounded many sutras....(continue to p.
176)....will approach Anuttara-samyak-sambodi"
R p. 229 "Then the Buddha spoke once again...(continue to top p.
230)...will come nearer to supreme awakening."

Relics of the Buddha vs. Teaching of the Buddha

After you have read the selection today split the remainder of
your practice time between practicing reading the Shindoku of
Chapter 16 as before and chanting Namu Myoho Renge Kyo.
You are also continuing to observe two of the Eight Right Ways
you selected to focus on. Hopefully you also are thinking about
your connections to others as you engage in some of your daily
activities.

As you think of your connections I wonder if you consider the
artist who designed any packaging for any of your food
products or other items you buy? Do you think of the
advertising departments that crafted the advertisements that
may have influenced your purchases either now or in the past?
How about the janitor in the bank that keeps your money safe
or even processes your card transactions, then there is the
security guard who refills the ATM if you used that, or the
guard that picks up the money from the store daily so that the
store is able to process payments. As you see the list can go on
for quite some time. See if you can think of some other more
obscure connections you may not have previously thought
about.

In the reading for today there are a couple of things I would like to call your attention to which may have escaped your consideration. One is the term 'Anuttara-samyak-sambodhi' as Murano has it or 'supreme awakening' as Reeves terms it. The other is did you catch the transition moment in the last paragraph of today's reading from remains of the Buddha to a copy of the sutra?

The term Anuttara-samyak-sambodhi actually appears for the first time in the Lotus Sutra. We will read about this in the selection for tomorrow but I wanted to mention it today so you can be observant to it. Previous to the Lotus Sutra the goal of Buddhist practice had been the attainment of Nirvana. But with the Lotus Sutra the Buddha says that actually Nirvana was just an expedient in order to cause people to begin to practice, it was never the ultimate goal, just one step along the way, so to speak. You'll read this tomorrow.

Today however in the last paragraph you read there occurs one of several key transition moments in the Lotus Sutra. I like to celebrate and mark these because they are points when the Buddha's teaching move to newer levels, or take a different turn than previously.

Today the Buddha tells us that the veneration of relics of the Buddha, or the body of the Buddha is being replaced by veneration of the teaching of the Buddha. It is the Dharma that now occupies the primary focus of our attention. It really always has been but the Buddha makes it clear so there can be no doubt.

In a way the beginning of the Lotus Sutra has been preparing us for this moment, especially when the Buddha said things like he would reveal the purpose for the appearance of any Buddha throughout time. Or statements like replacing the Three Vehicles with the Single Vehicle.

The 'perfect body' of the Buddha exists within the contents of the Sutra, specifically the Lotus Sutra being taught at this point. Here at the temple we have a stupa erected in the front with this passage written on it as well as the Odaimoku, Namu Myoho Renge Kyo.

I hope that you also realize that as you chant Namu Myoho Renge Kyo and study the Lotus Sutra you are erecting a stupa of seven treasures within your life.

DAY 17

Read Lotus Sutra
M p. 176 "Medicine-King! Although many.....(continue to p. 177 end of paragraph)....cause them to attain Anuttara-samyak-sambodhi."
R p. 230 first paragraph "Medicine King, thought there are many....(read three paragraphs on this page ending with)....the Buddha has opened it up."

Thirsty Man

Continue today splitting your remaining practice time between chanting Namu Myoho Renge Kyo and practicing reciting Chapter 16 in the Shindoku as before. Perhaps by this time you are feeling a little more confident in your reciting of Chapter 16 and may even be getting further along, some may even be able to recite the entire portion. Regardless, though, of how far you are getting, do not be discouraged or over confident. Take it slowly and deliberately, remember it is a meditative practice and as such should be done with mindfulness.

As you have been doing for the past several days continue developing your awareness to connections you have with people throughout the world who make your everyday living possible. Try to generate a real sense of appreciation for all those efforts, even if you do not know the specific individuals. And keep working on the two right ways you have selected to focus on. Make a mental note of your progress or where you fall short. This mental note taking is not meant to discourage you but to help you focus more attention on what needs work.

There is a really short parable here of a thirsty man. We previously ran across a starving man, and now we meet his counterpart the thirsty man. In this short story the thirsty man is digging in the ground for water to satisfy himself. When he was digging out dry earth he had no hope of finding water, but when he found moist earth he was encouraged to continue digging. He then finds mud and he becomes convinced that water must be near.

Before we came into contact with the Lotus Sutra, we were like digging in dry earth, never sure if enlightenment was a possibility, or if even happiness was possible. Yet as we read the Lotus Sutra, we have been encouraged first by moist earth with the early predictions of enlightenment and now we are actually digging up wet mud. In these paragraphs we see that those who practice in the time after the death of the Buddha and who carry out the five practices outlined are guaranteed to attain an enlightenment that had never been revealed before. This enlightenment is greater than the Nirvana that previously had been sought after.

This sutra that we are reading and studying every day is the sutra that casts aside all of the expedients, all the temporary teachings, all of the teachings designed to lead to this Anuttara-samyak-sambohi or supreme awakening. This sutra opens wide the gate, that up until now had been closed and limiting to Nirvana and show what is beyond that gate, and now makes it possible for all living beings to equally become enlightened.

I am not sure if you are as excited about this as it makes me, perhaps you are or perhaps it will develop in time. Either way, I hope you will continue your practice day by day without becoming discouraged or giving up. We have some really fantastic things in store for us in the next few chapters. We are now roughly half way through our 35 Days, congratulations.

DAY 18

Read Lotus Sutra
M p. 181 Beginning of Chapter XI to end of first paragraph p. 183
"Thereupon a stupa of the seven treasures ..... We wish to see that Buddha."
R p. 235 Beginning of Chapter XI to end of last full paragraph p. 236 "At that time a stupa of the seven precious....we want to see this Buddha's body."

Stupa of Many Treasures

I hope that the portion you will read today won't be too long for you. Please spend the remainder of your practice time today chanting Namu Myoho Renge Kyo. As before continue to work on your connections to the many people who make it possible for you to do the things you do in your life. Continue also, working on the two Right Ways that you have selected to focus on. You might take some time to also write out ways in which you have been successful in following the two chosen Right Ways.

Today I would like to encourage you to select one activity that you engage in during your day and add chanting Namu Myoho Renge Kyo while you do that activity. So for example you might perhaps choose driving. So beginning today every time you drive, as much as you can remember to do so chant Namu Myoho Renge Kyo while driving. It might be walking, or it might be washing dishes or some other thing. As before when you catch your mind wandering while doing this activity say the word 'thinking' to yourself and come back to your chanting.

Of course be safe in whatever activity you choose to do this practice.

Today in our reading something really phenomenal has happened. A huge stupa, or mausoleum has arisen from beneath the ground and appeared hanging in the sky above the congregation. The size of this structure is huge. I did a rough calculation once and it works out to be between roughly one fourth to one half the diameter of the earth in height. This stupa, because it is decorated with seven different treasure is called the stupa of treasures.

As you read, a loud voice, it would have to be loud to be heard, praises the Buddha saying; "Excellent, excellent!" and says that the Buddha Sakyamuni, has expounded the Lotus Sutra and that it is all true. A phenomenon such as this has not occurred at any time before in the teachings of the Buddha. Those in the congregation are amazed, as I am sure we all would be if we witnessed something of this magnitude.

The Buddha then explains why this stupa has appeared and who is on the inside. He tells us that a Buddha from a long time ago, an ancient Buddha, once made a vow that whenever and wherever the Lotus Sutra is taught he would cause his remains and mausoleum to appear in the presence of the teaching of the Lotus Sutra and declare its validity.

Nichiren, in many of his writings referred to the seven treasures as the seven characters that make up devotion to the Lotus Sutra, as written in Chinese

南無妙法蓮華経

or Namu Myoho Renge Kyo. These seven characters are written down the center of our Gohonzon Mandala and form the basis of our object of veneration.

Today is a lot to absorb. Let me leave you with this final thought. This object that has appeared before the congregation is phenomenal and seemingly impossible to have happened. Nichiren was quite clear about the possibility of manifesting this from within our own individual lives. As with all the teachings in the Lotus Sutra, they become real when we ourselves begin to change and reveal the truth from within our lives. Through chanting Namu Myoho Renge Kyo and following the practices given in the Lotus Sutra and applying the teachings in our lives we can reveal the truth of the teachings in our own unique ways. The treasure tower is none other than our own lives.

DAY 19

Read Lotus Sutra
M p. 183 "Many-Treasures Buddha
made another great
vow....(continue to top of page
187).....I have come to hear this
sutra direct from you."
R p. 236 "The Buddha said to Great
Delight....(continue to almost end of
page 239)....I have come to this
place to hear."

Purification of the World

Today I have given you a very
long portion to read. If you have any time remaining please
chant Namu Myoho Renge Kyo. If you have used all of your
practice time reading please do not worry, just chant Namu
Myoho Renge Kyo three times and conclude you formal
practice. As always throughout the day observe your two Right
Ways and connections mindfulness practices. Also as you
began yesterday continue with your selected activity during
which you are chanting Namu Myoho Renge Kyo silently to
yourself.

I apologize for giving you such a long reading assignment. I
considered breaking it all apart to shorten it, but I felt that
would make it too disjointed and might loose the effect.

You might wonder why reading this is so important. Let me see if I can briefly explain some things to consider about the passage you just read.

Have you ever wondered why there were so many Buddhas? Maybe you didn't even realize there were a lot, or maybe you never gave it any thought, or maybe you were confused. At any rate there are many different Buddhas in Buddhism, yet there is truly only one. In the portion we just read you may have noticed a term in the Murano translation called "Buddhas of his replicas" and in Reeves called "embodiments of that Buddha". Both of these are referring to the many manifestation or concepts of Buddha that are revealed in various other sutras.

In the Lotus Sutra, in this passage, we have the revelation of the unification of all the various names and personages of the various Buddhas as being the Single Buddha. We see that the purpose of these various manifestations is so that an appropriate Buddha for the needs of the various peoples is teaching Buddhism. The Buddhism they are all independently teaching though is actually leading to the Single Great Teaching of the Lotus Sutra. As we have read previously, there are many ways that Buddhism is taught, but there is only one truth and as the Buddha says, that truth is revealed in the Lotus Sutra.

Ok, beyond that, and that is a major concept, why did I suggest you read about all the purifications that take place and the calling back of all these various representation of the one Buddha?

The way I like to teach this is being similar to what we engage in every day as part of our daily practice, though I have not mentioned it previously.

Every day as we begin our practice we are encouraged to prepare our sacred space, hopefully you either have one already or are considering creating one for yourself. At any

72

rate as you begin your practice from today forward you should prepare your space by freshening it up, dusting, clearing away dead flowers or old offerings of fruit and such. You might be offering water, which is traditional, in which case you offer fresh water.

In a way I hope you equate this to the purification the Buddha does in this chapter. You are preparing the wonderful ground on which your practice occurs. Also, as you purify your physical space I hope you consider your mental or spiritual space as well. Focus on eliminating any distractions you may have going around in your head, the considerations of chores of the day or even what has occurred previously.

In a way, these are your emanations, your reflections, and your replicas. They are little mental pieces of yourself that are off some place doing some thing on your behalf. As you prepare to do your daily service, bring them all home, call them back to yourself and focus your entire mind and body on practicing in this moment in this space Buddhism.

This may be a new way of considering your daily practice and it will take practice. Please know that this is important. That is why I had you read this entire portion today.

Please be well!

DAY 20

Read Lotus Sutra
M p. 187 "Having see that the Buddha....(continue on same page)....to someone so that this sutra may be preserved."
R p. 239 "Then the four groups.... (continue to page 240) ....Wonderful Dharma Flower Sutra to someone."

Two Buddhas Sitting Side-by-Side

Today the reading is much shorter than it was yesterday but what you read today is very important, so please read it slowly and deliberately. After you have finished the reading today before you begin chanting spend 3 to 5 minutes and just sit with your feelings about what you have just read. Let it sink in for a while. Once you have done this spend the remainder of your time chanting Namu Myoho Renge Kyo.

There are three major things that occur in this short section. One is Many Treasures Buddha offers the seat beside him to Shakyamuni Buddha who then takes that seat. Two is Shakyamuni Buddha raises the congregation into the air so they can be on eye level with the two Buddhas. Three the Buddha asks those present who will teach the Lotus Sutra in the Saha-World, this world, so that it may be preserved?

Previously I had mentioned that the characters Namu Myoho Renge Kyo down the center of our Gohonzon, the object of veneration of the Lotus Sutra, represent the Stupa of Many Treasures. Just to the left and right of Namu Myoho Renge Kyo are the Two Buddhas, Shakyamuni and Many Treasures.

Sometimes this is depicted in statues it is also depicted in calligraphic form on a paper Mandala.

Previously I had talked about transition moments and this is another of those. At this point the entire congregation is now in the air and this is called the second location of thee that occur in the Lotus Sutra. It is also a transition moment that reinforces one that occurred previously, and that is the shift from the present to the future with regard to propagation and protection of the Sutra.

Here also we have the unification of the past Buddha with the present Buddha, both of whom are looking toward the future. So the focus really shifts firmly to the future of Buddhism and who will practice and spread the Dharma in the ages after the death of the Buddha.

This passage has some profound philosophical importance that I can not fully address here in this short introduction so I hope you will contact your teacher to further explore this. You may also listen or read some of my lectures on the Lotus Sutra for further information.

Continue in your practice of following your two Right Ways and your focus on connections to the many beings that make various aspects of your life possible. Also remember to continue your chanting during some of your daily activities.

It is important to as deeply as possible connect your life with chanting Namu Myoho Renge Kyo so that the Lotus Sutra is never far from your thoughts.

DAY 21

Read Lotus Sutra
M p. 190 "Good men! Think this
over clearly!...(continue to end of
chapter)"
R p. 243 "All my good
sons....(continue to the end of the
chapter)"

Nine Difficult and Six Easy Things

After you finish reading today's selection divide your time between chanting Namu Myoho Renge Kyo and reading Chapter 16 in Shindoku. Congratulations, today is the end of 3 weeks of practicing and studying the Lotus Sutra. I hope it hasn't been too difficult for you.

Speaking of difficult, what did you think about the reading today? The portion we read today has two parts to it, though you may not have been aware of it. The first part is the Nine Difficult and Six Easy Things. The second part is called Hotoge or Difficulty of Retaining the Sutra. The first part begins where we began reading and ends at the top of page 193 in the Murano and end of third stanza on page 245 in the Reeves.

The Hotoge or Difficulty of Retaining the Sutra begins on page 193 with "It is difficult to keep this sutra..." in the Murano and page 246 with "This sutra is so difficult to embrace..." in the Reeves. Both continue to the end of the chapter.

In case it was not clear before reading this you should have a pretty good idea of three things. One is that it isn't easy to practice and keep this teaching of the Buddha. The second thing is that among all the sutras the Buddha taught, of all the teachings of the Buddha this one is the most important and also the hardest to observe. Finally, the third thing is by practicing, by following and embracing this Sutra a person will be praised by all the Buddhas and be able to attain enlightenment.

I am always somewhat amused when I read the list of difficult and easy things, because to me none of the easy things are easy at all. Yet I do know that practicing the Lotus Sutra is hard to do, especially over a lifetime. But slowly and surely I have managed to do so and it seems, when looking back quite beneficial. It is because I know it can be difficult that I am hoping this 35 day practice will be helpful to you in establishing a pattern in your life to help you continue your practice long into the future.

Today, as you prepare for beginning the third week of practice I encourage you to write down some things that you may have noticed that appear to hinder your practice. Write down things like "I get busy", or "I sleep too late" or "I am too tired", or even "It is too confusing". Whatever the obstacle is write it down, try to do so without guilt, and try not to have too much remorse. Just be honest, that is also a key practice in Buddhism, to get to know ourselves in a frank and honest manner so that we can begin to work on changing the things that are preventing us from becoming happy.

Once you have written down anything that stands in your way to daily practice you can confront it. Consider it as you go through your day. See if you can dig deeper into what about that thing is actually the cause of not practicing. Again try to engage in this exercise with honesty and with out shame or guilt. The facts are what they are, but by looking at them we can begin to change those things. If we ignore it then no change will occur.

As you consider the things that stand in your way to practice see if you notice a pattern. In the Nine Difficult and Six Easy Things you may have noticed that the nine difficult things are of a mental/spiritual nature and the six easy things are of a physical nature. This shows us that it is sometimes the most difficult of things to change, those things that reside in our mind, our spirit, or our emotions. Does this help you to see your obstacle differently?

As in the days before also continue to work on your two Right Ways as well as your connections to countless other beings.

DAY 22

Read Lotus Sutra
M p. 195 "In those days the lives of the people...(continue to end
of first paragraph p. 196)....be short of anything."
M p. 197 "The king at that time was...(continue to first sentence
of last paragraph)...Devadatta will become a Buddha after
innumerable kalpas."
M p. 201 "Thereupon Sariputra said to the daughter...(continue
to end of chapter)"
R p. 247 "At that time a person's lifetime...(continue to end of the
page 247)"
R p. 249 "The Buddha said to the monks:...(continue to first
sentence of next paragraph)"
R p. 252 "Then Shariputra said to the dragon girl...(continue to
end of chapter)"

Devadatta and The Dragon King's Daughter

Congratulations on beginning your fourth week of practice.
You have accomplished something very noteworthy, I hope you
are pleased so far with what you have accomplished. I hope
that practicing is becoming easier and you are enjoying reading
and exploring the Lotus Sutra.

How are you doing on your Right Ways? You may have
guessed already, however in case you have not today I
encourage you to add a third one to what you are focusing on.
Maybe if you have not already done so write them down on a
card and put them some place you will see them, perhaps your
altar or even your bathroom mirror. The practice of Buddhism

never really ends, as you may have surmised, there is always work for us to do.

After you finish today's reading divide your time between chanting and reading as much of the Shindoku of Chapter 16 as you are able. Has the reading of the Shindoku become any easier? It may not, yet. It is alright though just do the best you are able. The most significant improvement will probably only come if you are able to practice along with others. There are many ways you can accomplish this, one of course is if you live near a temple or practice group you can join with them. Another option is to seek out a temple that is broadcasting their services on the Internet; there are several who do. Another option is to speak with your teacher about a recording of the chanting of the sutra.

Today we read two sections from Chapter XII, titled Devadatta. In case you are not familiar with this person, he is the cousin of the Buddha. He is noteworthy or remembered because of his multiple attempts to kill the Buddha as well as his attempt to split the Sangha. In his attempt to split the Sangha he also tried to pervert or distort the teachings of the Buddha. So, he is notorious for causing harm to each of the Three Jewels of Buddhism; the Buddha, the Dharma, and the Sangha.

In the first short section we learn of the deep connection that existed between the Buddha and this person who sought to destroy Buddhism. We learn that the Buddha praises this person who has done so much evil saying that because of their relationship in the past the Buddha was able to become the Buddha.

I wonder how many of us can look at those who cause us grief and thank them for the growth opportunities they provide us. It isn't easy to express appreciation for such opportunities. Normally we just want to avoid at all cost those things that bother us.

Or perhaps we may want to seek out only pleasurable things or the easy way. Yet in doing the easy things we don't always grow in the same way as if we were to challenge ourselves. You have chosen to try something of great difficulty, you have chosen to challenge your life. You are to be commended for this effort, and you should know that without doubt your life is changing, even if you don't yet see it.

Finally in the last portion of our reading today there is the story of the Dragon Kings Daughter who even though she is female and as stated has what is known as the Five Impossibilities she effortlessly becomes a Buddha.

In this one chapter we see proof that the worst of the worst can become Buddhas and that also all beings are able to attain enlightenment. In the time of the Buddha women were not thought to be equal to men. Even still in our modern time there are many who would deny equality to women, even preventing them from religious offices. In this chapter we see that from the time of the Buddha such revolutionary concepts as equality was taught.

Today, as you add one more Right Way to your list of daily practice also continue working on connections in various areas of your daily life. Finally, when we began I asked you to write down something about yourself you might like to change. Do you still have that? I wonder how that is going? Have you noticed even a slight change? If not do not become discouraged, the change will happen, in fact it probably already has, even if the change is being more self aware.

Congratulations again on beginning week four!

DAY 23

Read Lotus Sutra
M p. 206 "Do not worry!...(continue to end of chapter)"
R p. 257 "Please do not worry....(continue to end of chapter)"

Three Powerful Enemies

After you have concluded the reading today split the remainder of your practice time between chanting Namu Myoho Renge Kyo and the Shindoku of Chapter 16. It won't be long now and we will get to the English of this portion that you are reading in Shindoku.

As before, continue throughout the day to try to follow now your three Right Ways. Also how is the work going on addressing the obstacles you have to your daily practice? Don't worry; we all have some difficulty that tries to stand in the way of our daily efforts.

In the section we read today it talks about some of the external factors that can stand in the way or try to prevent us from practicing. You may not directly face any of these challenges, but you might. Perhaps there is a family member who discounts or challenges or even ridicules your practice. Or maybe a co-worker gives you a hard time once they found out you are trying to practice Buddhism. In some cases perhaps a religious person is challenging your practice.

These kinds of problems are not unheard of and not rare, so please do not feel alone if you face this.

Nichiren, the found of Nichiren Buddhism who so dedicatedly taught and practiced the Lotus Sutra in the 13th Century suffered repeated persecutions as did many of his contemporary followers. In one of his famous writings he cites these passages from the Lotus Sutra as proof that what was happening to him was to be expected and was predicted in the Lotus Sutra.

Way back when I first began practicing I was in the military, which at that time was not the most favorable circumstances. Sometimes it was even hostile to my practice. I hope that you do not have to endure any such difficulties. For me it was encouraging to read Nichiren's writings and study the Sutra to see that these things may happen and to not become discouraged.

So why do we do it? I mean wouldn't it be easier to practice some other religion or to just give up? These are personal questions and each person needs to find the answer within. We can of course read passages such as these in the Sutra, and we can find encouragement by doing so, but still the desire to continue has to well up from inside your own life.

I think at times such as when we are facing a difficult situation we have an opportunity to really internalize the teachings of the Buddha. All at once it becomes not so much of an intellectual endeavor as one rooted deep down reaching the core of our lives.

It is at times like those when we can really understand what it means to take on the Buddha's mantle and try to teach others of the greatness of Buddhism as we have read in the Lotus Sutra.

I do hope though that your practice is not so difficult though, but there will certainly be times when you will be challenged. Do not become discouraged, and don't forget what you have studied in the Lotus Sutra.

Remember, your three Right Ways, your connections and of course continue to chant Namu Myoho Renge Kyo throughout your day when you are able.

DAY 24

Read Lotus Sutra
M p. 221 "Manjusri! I will tell you a parable...(continue to p.
222)...Now I expound it to you today for the first time."
R p. 271 "Majushri, it is like a powerful...(continue to p.
272)...Today for the first time I lay it out for all of you."

Gem In The Top-Knot

At the conclusion of your reading today continue to split your time remaining between chanting Namu Myoho Renge Kyo and reading the Shindoku of a the portion of Chapter 16 we have been working on. Also, you guessed it, keep working on the Right Ways you have selected to focus on. Throughout your day I also hope you are continuing to chant Namu Myoho Renge Kyo to yourself whenever you are able.

Chanting Namu Myoho Renge Kyo silently to yourself may seem like it is a superfluous or unimportant practice, but I don't think this is true. There are several benefits to be obtained by doing this practice. One obvious one is that it constantly brings to your mind that you are trying to practice Buddhism with your whole life, not just as some temporary or intellectual activity.

A further benefit is that you are ever more deeply embracing the heart and core of the teaching of the Lotus Sutra, even in ways you may not be fully aware of yet. Just as it isn't necessary for you to fully understand the complexities of many devices you use daily such as TV or phone or even radio or the internet in order to benefit from them, so too with Buddhism.

Your internal practice of chanting Namu Myoho Renge Kyo connects you with the spirit, or as I mentioned the core, of the teaching of the Lotus Sutra.

Also, chanting Namu Myoho Renge Kyo is a meditative practice so it has physiological benefits as well, such as lowering your blood pressure and heart rate. It also helps to clear the mind of many distracting thoughts enabling your innate wisdom or your Buddha wisdom to rise to the surface. So please do your best to chant whenever possible.

Today the reading covered a short little parable called gem in the top-knot. At first reading you may wonder what a king going to war has to do with the Buddha. As we read further though we see that indeed the Buddha was like this king, because he fought the forces of Mara, the king Devil.

Right before the Buddha attained his enlightenment as he sat under the tree he was confronted with the demon forces of Mara who tried to prevent him from becoming enlightened, and thereby enabling all mankind to break the bonds of suffering. The Buddha was able to defeat the vast resources Mara threw at him, and finally attained enlightenment.

We too, must overcome our own Mara, those things that arise in our minds to try to become discouraged and give up our Buddhist practice. Previously I talked about those things that occur in our environment to try to prevent us from practicing, today we deal with the obstacles occurring in our mind. These obstacles may be in the form of doubts such as our self-worth or our personal ability to become enlightened. It also may be doubts about the truth of Buddhism, or doubts about the value of practicing. We all experience these moments when we may think things impossible or not worth it.

Being aware of the workings of our minds is the first step to overcoming these kinds of difficulties. Mara isn't so much of a real thing as it is a figurative example or a personification of those things in our mind that prevent us from becoming happy or enlightened.

The Buddha says in this portion of the Sutra that up until this point he has held back, he has kept in reserve the most valuable, the most important teaching of Buddhism; that being the Lotus Sutra. He tells us that this Sutra is where the greatest treasure of the Buddhas is kept, that it is superior to all the other Sutras ever taught.

This may seem like a bold statement, but there is merit to it, if for no other reason than contained within the Lotus Sutra are teachings that have not occurred previously in any of the other Sutras. Yet we have not even reached the last of those unique and first teachings. Some of those firsts that we have read so far include; the size of the congregation, the numerous deities in attendance, the predictions of enlightenment for people who had previously been denied enlightenment, the enlightenment of plants and animals, and the enlightenment of women.

Regarding the enlightenment of women, the day before we read of the daughter of the Dragon King. Yesterday, in a portion that we did not read, there was also the enlightenment of Gautami and Yasodhara, the aunt of the Buddha and the Buddha's wife, thus women are clearly included in enlightenment where before they had been excluded. This was a very revolutionary teaching!

I hope you have a joy filled day. Tomorrow we have something very exciting happening and something with great implications to our lives.

DAY 25

Read Lotus Sutra
M p. 228 "No good men!...(continue to p. 230)...Do they not fatigue you?"
M p. 233 "These Bodhisattvas have...(continue to p. 234)..."Remove our doubts!"
M p. 236 "Ajita, know this, these great Bodhisattvas...(continue to p. 237)..."Since the remotest past."
M p. 238 "It is not long...(continue to end of chapter)"
R p. 279 "Then the Buddha said...(continue to bottom p. 280)...make the World-Honored One tired?"
R p. 284 "In all four regions...(continue to end of p. 284)...Please dispel the doubts of this congregation!"
R p. 286 "Ajita, you should know...(continue to p. 287)...I have been teaching and transforming this multitude."
R p. 289 "In the past the Buddha...(continue to end of chapter)"

Bodhisattvas From Underground

Today there was a lot to read. I asked you to jump around a bit in this chapter because I did not want to break up this into two days. I felt it would be better experienced as one days worth of reading. I hope it worked well for you. There is still much of the chapter that was not read but you were able to

93

read the highlights, which for now is satisfactory, especially for the kind of exposure we are trying for in this short period.

As has been the practice in previous days please spend the remainder of your practice time chanting Namu Myoho Renge Kyo. As you chant I would like for you to see if you can call up any images you may have in your mind that connect with the reading.

What did you think as you were reading the selections today? Did you have some of the same questions as the folks present in the congregation have? Who are these people who have now suddenly appeared rising from the ground?

There are a couple of things I would like to point out to you. The first is the four leaders who you read about on M p. 230 and R p. 280. These four leaders are also depicted on the Gohonzon either as statues or as calligraphic names on the paper Mandala. In statue form they are four identical statues with only slight differences in robe colors and in calligraphic form they appear on the first line flanking the names of Many Treasures Buddha and Shakyamuni Buddha.

A second thing I always like to point out is how these people who have risen from underground approach the Buddha. There is a stark contrast between their behavior and the behavior of the Buddha's contemporary disciples. Unlike the Buddha's contemporary disciples who have asked for personal predictions of enlightenment, these folks who came from underground ask the Buddha about his health and well-being.

The Bodhisattvas who arise from underground do not ask for things for themselves, their concern is for the Buddha. The contemporaries of the Buddha seek for their own selves and do not ask the Buddha how he is doing. There is a definite shift in concern. One group is concerned for themselves, the other is concerned for others. Did you notice that? Perhaps you didn't since our reading has been jumping around so much, that is why I am pointing it out to you.

As we read about these new people who have just risen from beneath the ground we see that they are in many respects just like the Buddha. M p. 233 and R p. 284 we see many of the same phenomena that occurred as the Buddha began teachings this Lotus Sutra, the ground quaking. We also see that these Bodhisattvas have divine and supernatural powers, they are clearly different from the contemporaries of the Buddha.

We learn that these Bodhisattvas have a long-term relationship with the Buddha. They have been trained by, and have practiced diligently under the Buddha for countlessly long periods of time. The Buddha calls them his sons.

Finally, among the things I would like to point you to today is the fact that the Buddha has now declined the offer of various folks to spread the Dharma in the future ages after his death, and instead is giving that responsibility to this new group of people. This is a key point because of how it relates to those of us who practice the Lotus Sutra in this current day and age.

Since we are in the time after the death of the Buddha, and since we are practicing, studying, and teaching this sutra, just as the Buddha instructs us, then who might we most be like of all the people in the Lotus Sutra? The Buddha says that it is the Bodhisattvas who have just appeared from underground who will be the people who practice, study and teach the Lotus Sutra in the ages after his death, so might we just possibly be representing these Bodhisattvas from underground? Might we not actually be the very people who the Buddha has trained to do this from the remotest past?

This process of asking these questions and finding the answers in our own lives is actually part of the transference of the responsibility for the protection of the Lotus Sutra that occurs here and in subsequent chapters of the Lotus Sutra. As we continue in our practice, as we develop a greater understanding of the Lotus Sutra, our relationship to the Lotus Sutra changes from one of a historical perspective to one of a current contemporary relationship.

No longer is this an almost 3000-year-old teaching it now becomes a story of our own lives. This is part of the process of an ever-deepening understanding, and embracing of the Lotus Sutra. At first, as we approach the Lotus Sutra it is as a study of what has happened in the past to an accounting of what is actually happening right now in our own lives.

This may escape you at the present time, but it is good to be aware of the fact the Lotus Sutra is really a story about your own life and your long-term relationship to the Buddha that spans past, present, and future.

There is a lot to absorb today. And this is a life-long process, one of an ever deepening realization.

Today as in days past, continue your chanting of Namu Myoho Renge Kyo as you engage in your daily activities and continue to work on now three of your Right Ways as well as your connections to others for your life.

In many ways today begins the arising of your own life, even though you have been practicing chanting Namu Myoho Renge Kyo up until today you may have not known of your actual place within the Lotus Sutra. You are actually written about in this chapter of the Lotus Sutra your story is here.

DAY 26

Read Lotus Sutra
M p. 246 "It is many hundreds of thousands...(continue to end of chapter)"
R p. 295 "Since I became a Buddha...(continue to end of chapter)"

Eternal Buddha

Finally we have come to the single most important portion of the Lotus Sutra. This is also the English of what you have been reading or practicing reading in Shindoku, the liturgical language. Unlike in some of the more dramatic sections we have read in the past few days, this section may seem rather ordinary. It is not ordinary though, and is quite dramatic, even if in an understated way.

After you have finished reading the section today, go back now and try reading the Shindoku version you have been working on. When you have finished reading both of them if you have any time remaining please spend it chanting Namu Myoho Renge Kyo.

In this chapter, in the section we have read, as well as in more detail in the portion we did not read, we learn of the eternal, always existing nature of 'Buddha'. The Buddha says that he is always present that he has always been present and that he will always be present. There is really no such thing as a temporary phenomena of Buddha, such as represented by a historical figure.

As I said, this is rather understated and less dramatic than some of the things we have been reading, yet the idea of the

Buddha always existing is a dramatic shift from a concept of Buddha being just one historical figure. We have shifted the focus of Buddha from a single man represented by, in our world's case Shakyamuni, to a concept of Buddha spanning time and place.

Nichiren taught that this one section of the Lotus Sutra is actually the eye of the Sutra and there are six reasons for its superiority.

These six reasons are:
1.) Eternity of Buddhas
2.) Shows people the way to Buddhahood
3.) Expresses the eternal Buddha Land
4.) The timeless salvation or enlightenment of people
5.) The actual enlightenment or saving of people of all ages, and
6.) The original and always active vow of all Buddhas.

These are rather important ideas that have never been expressed or revealed in any of the Buddha's previous teachings.

I think one important idea to try to grasp today, as you are first exposed to this teaching is there is no other place more perfect to practice than the place in which we reside. That this place we are in, is actually the Buddha's Pure Land, but that manifestation is up to us to realize. Also, as I mentioned yesterday we have an infinite connection not with the historical person Shakyamuni but with a concept of Buddhahood as Bodhisattvas from Underground.

When we are separated from, or distance ourselves from, the eternal truth of Buddhahood we will tend to see our lives, our existence, as one separate from enlightenment, we will see our world as one of strife and suffering. However, if we see ourselves as having an always existing connection to, and with the eternal concept of Buddhahood, then we can see the Buddha manifest in our lives and in our environment.

The Buddha is not merely someone who lived, taught, and perished some 2500 or so years ago. But as taught in the Lotus Sutra, the Buddha is actually a presence in the life and environment that spans time or place. The Buddha taught in the Lotus Sutra that there is really no fundamental difference between the enlightenment he attained and the enlightenment that resides within our lives. The real difference is how we relate to it and whether or not we choose to manifest it.

All of this is a rather deep and profound teaching. This one section gets to the heart of what we are trying to realize in our daily lives. It is the core of our practice and effort. I also believe that it is a life-long endeavor.

What I have written today is just a short humble attempt at putting into a few words something that is way larger than these words can convey. I hope that you will connect with your teacher and explore this in greater depth

Please continue on with your chanting Namu Myoho Renge Kyo as you go about your day. Also continue to explore your connections to countless other living beings for your very existence, this is mindfulness practice. We are in our final ten days of this practice and study. You have come a long way since you have begun, you should be proud of what you have accomplished so far, you are fulfilling the vows of countless lifetimes of relationships with the Buddha.

DAY 27

Read Lotus Sutra
M p. 254 "Ajita! Anyone who hears that my life is so long...(continue to end paragraph)"
M p. 259 "Anyone who reads, recites, or keeps this sutra...(continue to end of paragraph)"
M p. 263 "Ajita! Suppose a bhiksu...(continue to end of paragraph)"
M p. 282 "Furthermore, Constant-Endeavor!...(continue to end of paragraph)
R p. 305 "Then the Buddha said...(continue to end of paragraph)"
R p. 310 "If, for the sake of others...(continue to end of paragraph)"
R p. 315 "Then the Buddha said...(continue to end of paragraph)"
R p. 333 "Furthermore, Constant Effort,...(continue to end of paragraph)"

Merits of Person 50 Removed

Today I have selected four paragraphs from the three next chapters which all deal with the merit, or benefits that will accrue to those who practice this Lotus Sutra, especially in the ages after the death of the Buddha. After you have finished reading these paragraphs please divide your remaining time between reciting the portion of Chapter 16 in Shindoku and chanting Namu Myoho Renge Kyo.

In the first paragraph of today's selections the Buddha talks about the importance of understanding or even considering the longevity of the life of the Buddha. The Buddha says, that compared to practicing the Six Paramitas, or the Six Perfections, understanding and believing in the long life of the Buddha is far more beneficial.

You may probably be asking why is it so important, what relevance does it have to us, that the Buddha has told us of the infinite life-span of Buddha. One reason is because without this truth then there really is no teacher for the Bodhisattvas who rise up from beneath the ground, and there is no current relationship with the Buddha other than as a historical person.

Of course this is all nice theory, and of course it exists on paper in the sutra, but what our practice is fundamentally about is manifesting the truth of the matter in our own individual lives. As our faith, built upon practice, grows and we experience the proof of the Lotus Sutra in our lives our relationship with the Lotus Sutra, and also with this concept of an Eternal Buddha changes. It is no longer merely a theoretical idea but an actual experienced truth. This takes time of course, but during that time the Buddha assures us that the merit we accumulate is unimaginable, and far greater than possible by those who practice in the time of the Buddha, and for whom the belief in Eternal Buddha is not important.

If we look at the predictions of future enlightenment given to the contemporaries of the Buddha we see that they will become enlightened at some future point because of their relationship with the historical Buddha, Shakyamuni. But those who teach and practice the Lotus Sutra after the death of the Buddha, the Bodhisattvas from Underground, have a relationship with the Buddha that spans far into the infinite past and because of this they have already attained great supernatural powers and all the marks of the Buddha.

The Bodhisattvas from Underground do not come into this Saha World, this world of sufferings, in order to practice so that they can become enlightened, they come into this world after the time of the Buddha so they can teach others to become enlightened. These Bodhisattvas from Underground have already achieved a far greater practice than those contemporaries of the historical Buddha.

Of course, it is up to each of us as we practice to reveal this truth in our own unique capacities through our continued practice of the Lotus Sutra.

Just as the Bodhisattvas from Underground emerged from beneath the ground, we too emerge from our seemingly mundane lives and reveal the Buddha that is within us.

Finally today I would like to talk a little about the benefit or merit of the 50th person removed, which you read of in Chapter 18. In the single paragraph appearing at the beginning of this chapter we read about rejoicing. This idea of rejoicing is extremely important, I believe.

Specifically this paragraph talks about the benefit that will accrue to the fiftieth person who hears even indirectly about the joy of practicing the Lotus Sutra by the first person. That is how powerful a teaching the Lotus Sutra is and it is also an expression of how powerful joy is.

When we chant Namu Myoho Renge Kyo we are engaging in a very profound activity. Many of have come into Buddhism from a Judeo-Christian perspective, even if only remotely. For some of us the concept of prayer is an activity of asking for something, of seeking for some intercession by some force outside of our lives. Of course this is not to say that all religions or that all people pray in such a way, but it certainly common.

In Buddhism and especially as we chant Namu Myoho Renge Kyo we are engaging not in this manner of praying but from the perspective of praising the Lotus Sutra, of celebrating the truths contained within this teaching of the Buddha, and of rejoicing. Our praying is not about something coming into our lives or something being done for our lives, our praying is about the changes that take place in our lives because of our practice and our celebration of those changes.

Joy and gratitude are fundamental practices of Buddhism. We say Namu because we appreciate our lives, we appreciate our practice and relationship to the Lotus Sutra or Myoho Renge Kyo. Namu is an expression of our relationship to the Lotus Sutra. Namu is not a question, it is not a seeking for something outside our lives, Namu is an expression of what is already in our lives and our ever-deepening relationship to those truths. Namu is not '*I want this*', it is instead saying '*I am this*'.

These passages we read today reveal that because of the relationship we create with the Lotus Sutra we will be assured of great merit, the great merit of awakening what is already in our lives, Buddhahood. Frequently I have heard Namaste translated as the god in me bows to the god in you. And so it is when we append that to Myoho Renge Kyo. The Buddha in me bows to the Buddha in the Lotus Sutra.

Please consider this as you continue to chant Namu Myoho Renge Kyo throughout your day and as you work on your practice of following now three of the eight Right Ways. Remember to keep joy in your heart and share that joy with all the connections you become mindful of during your day. The joy you express is passed on and benefits countless others.

DAY 28

Read Lotus Sutra
M p. 289 "There was once a Buddha...(continue to end of chapter)"
R p. 340 "In the past there was a Buddha...(continue to end of chapter)"

Never Despising Bodhisattva

Yes, you guessed it; after you finish today's reading spend the remainder of your time split between chanting Namu Myoho Renge Kyo and reading the Shindoku of Chapter 16. As you chant today consider how difficult it is to respect every person we have contact with in our lives, even the people who bug us, or who sometimes may present difficult behaviors to us.

It was a tough choice today deciding on which section to read. One of the pitfalls of picking bits and pieces out of the Lotus Sutra for you to read is that much has been omitted. Up until this point I have not said, and it may not have been obvious to you, that what is presnted in the prose sections is repeated in the verse sections, though sometimes differently.

Frequently the verse sections repeat what the prose sections have, but with a slightly different twist. I think for the most part I have given you selections from the prose sections, which may not have been the most colorful and so you may have missed this. Each part is important and perhaps after you finish with this 35 day practice guide you will go back and read the selections that mirror what I have given you to read.

Today we read about a practitioner of the Lotus Sutra from the past who's sole practice, or who's sole expression of the Lotus Sutra was to bow to, respect, revere and praise all whom he came into contact with. In the course of praising them and honoring their eventual enlightenment, he faced criticism, abuse and hatred. He continued to follow this practice and not once did he respond in a negative way towards those who sought to cause him grief or harm.

If you are anything like me, this will be a difficult practice to follow. Sometimes it is difficult to see the good in people when they are presenting something otherwise. I think the idea of presenting is important because no one is all bad, it is just perhaps what we are seeing in them in the moment.

From the perspective of the Lotus Sutra, and as we have learned in our previous readings, everyone, regardless of the life condition they are presenting in this moment, has Buddhahood within their lives. Remember Devadatta, the cousin of the Buddha who tried to kill the Buddha and who tried to destroy the Sangha? Even this worst of the worst person is guaranteed to become a Buddha.

Whatever life a person may be manifesting in this moment does not diminish or deny their inherent Buddha, the Buddha of their enlightened life.

As practitioners of the Lotus Sutra you might say that our practice is to bow to everyone we meet so that we can awaken their Buddha within. Think of it in this way. When someone calls you by name you become alert and pay attention. So too when we bow to the Buddha in another, we are calling a wake-up to that Buddha potential within them. We are saying "hello, time to wake up."

This may sound crazy, but if you have Buddhahood within you, and you do, then so too does every other living being. Part of the reason why I have encouraged you to consider you connections to others, to consider your dependence on others was to help you develop an appreciation to the Buddha within other people, people you may not even be aware of. When you express appreciation for those efforts of others, when you can respect them you are calling out to the Buddha within them as well.

This section we read about is talking about a practice based upon relationship and also something called seed-planting. We create a relationship, or rather we become aware of the relationship that exists between ourselves and countless others and we praise that relationship and the other people we are connected to. We also plant the seeds to their own eventual awakening and we further nourish it by continually calling out to the Buddha in the other person.

So, as you carry on throughout your day today, continue contemplating your connections to the countless others and practice your four Right Ways. Also as you go through your day see if you can become aware of those times when it is difficult for you to praise the Buddha in other people.

DAY 29

Read Lotus Sutra
M p. 292 first two paragraphs
"Thereupon the Bodhisattva-
mahasattvas...make offerings to it."
M p. 294 "The Buddhas, the World-
Saviors, have...(continue to end of
chapter)"
M p. 297 "For many hundreds of
thousands...(continue to end of
paragraph)"
R p. 346 first two paragraphs "At
that time...radiating immeasurable
light."
R p. 347 "The Buddhas, the saviors of the world...(continue to end
of chapter)"
R p. 351 "In this way...(continue for two paragraphs)...repaid the
grace of the Buddhas."

Transmissions

Congratulations! Today begins the fifth and final week of this suggested 35 day practice outline. You might consider congratulating yourself for all that you have accomplished so far. You have almost read through portions, important portions of the Lotus Sutra and you have begun to develop a practice, which you can use as a foundation for your further lifetime of practice. You are accomplishing a great thing, something that fulfills the predictions in the Lotus Sutra and begins to repay your gratitude to the Buddha for his teachings.

If the Buddha had chosen to keep his enlightenment to himself, the people of today, ourselves included, may not have been given the door through which our own enlightenment would be possible. Further if the Buddha had failed to teach the Lotus Sutra then we of generations long after the Buddha would have no assurance that any practice or teaching of the Buddha would be appropriate specifically for us.

In no other teaching does the Buddha spend so much time and effort on a teaching for a time beyond his own lifetime, a teaching specifically for the ages when the effect of the Dharma would diminish.

Today we read of the great vow or promise the Bodhisattvas who arose from beneath the ground made to the Buddha to practice and teach the Lotus Sutra in ages after he died. We also read of the Buddhas transference of the teachings of the Lotus Sutra to future practitioners such as ourselves.

I should point out to you that the verse section of Chapter 21, which I had you, read is the place in the Lotus Sutra where Nichiren drew part of his name. The portion that reads 'just as the light of the sun..." is the first character in the name Nichiren. Nichi is the character for sun and ren is the character for renge or Lotus. So Nichiren's name means Sun Lotus.

The past few days I have written rather long entries, today I'll keep it a bit shorter. Before I wrap things up though, I would like to draw your attention to the closing of the portion of Chapter 22 I had you read. In that section the Buddha says that when we tell people about the Lotus Sutra they may not readily take faith or even be open to what we are sharing. This should not discourage us.

If they cannot accept the Lotus Sutra then we should share with them some other of the Buddha's teachings with the objective of causing them joy and benefit. So an example of

110

this would be to merely open their eyes to concepts such as cause and effect, or even dependent origination such as you have been working on throughout your practice in this outline. Or we might consider sharing teaching of equality, or even the benefit of the Eight Right Ways.

There are many things that we can introduce people to that are Buddhist concepts without even mentioning Buddhist terms. The concepts will benefit people as they live their lives and will actually cause them to plant roots of fortune to be able to take faith in some lifetime.

As Buddhist we should never loose sight of the infinite nature of life, that there is not just this lifetime but countless lifetimes and that eventually each person will manifest their inherent Buddha life.

Today you begin your fifth week. This would be a good time to take a look at the remaining Right Ways. As you look at them try to do so from the perspective of how much you have accomplished so far. One thing about these Right Ways is that as you work on a few, that work impacts the others and it becomes, even if slowly, easier to follow all the Right Ways.

Follow up your reading today by continuing your chanting of Namu Myoho Renge Kyo as well as reciting the portion of Chapter 16 in Shindoku. Continue your practice of chanting Namu Myoho Renge Kyo as much as you can throughout your daily activities.

Again congratulations on beginning your fifth week!

DAY 30

Read Lotus Sutra
M p. 304 "Star-King-Flower! Just as the sea is larger...(continue
to top page 306)...to the copy of this sutra."
R p. 358 "For example, Constellation-King Flower...(continue to
359)...the blessing obtained will also be innumerable."

Medicine King Bodhisattva

Just as in days past spend the remainder of your practice time
split between reciting the Shindoku of Chapter 16 and chanting
Namu Myoho Renge Kyo. I hope it is becoming easier for you
to read the Shindoku of Chapter 16, though I expect you are
still probably having some challenges. Please do not be
discouraged as for most people it takes a while to be able to
read it easily. Even being read poorly there is great merit to be
obtained, so don't feel like you are getting nowhere.

In this section we read today it talks about the incomparable
merits to be gained by practicing even a little bit of this Sutra. I
would like to point you to the sentence on page 305 in Murano
and 359 in Reeves where it says that just as a torch dispels
darkness this sutra saves all living beings from all sufferings.

Think about, if you will, a cave that has not seen any light in
thousands of years. In a single moment once a torch is brought
inside, the place is illuminated. It doesn't matter how dark or
for how long, the illumination is instant. It is the same with our
lives.

No matter how poorly we may think of our lives, or no matter how long we have been absent from the Lotus Sutra, the effect of a single moment of practice can cause us to remove accumulated sufferings. We may not think it is possible for such a thing, and we may not notice the changes right away, but they are taking place none-the-less.

Think about it this way. For the time you are chanting and practicing you are making a change in your thinking, even if only for a moment. Have you even noticed a rut in a patch of grass where people have been walking across? That dirt path or rut is an accumulation of many footsteps on the grass, which have caused the grass to die away, the ground to become hard, and inhospitable for the growth of grass.

When people stop walking across this patch of grass then the conditions are favorable for the grass to regrow. Still, however, the grass does not immediately return, though it will eventually. Our lives are the same; if we stop making bad causes then eventually over time our sufferings will diminish.

Going back to the patch of grass, if we not only stop walking on that section, but also loosen the ground up and plant some seeds, and water it, the grass will return faster. In our lives the same things occur when we begin to practice Buddhism.

We are not only more conscious of the causes we make but we are also loosening the dirt, which is the foundation of our unique lives. We begin to water and plant seeds with our practice. All the while as we continue to practice we keep tending to the grass, or our lives. By practicing Buddhism we can nourish the good things in our lives, the things that will result in the greatest joy, and we begin to eliminate the things that cause us suffering.

Even though, going back to our patch of grass, we may not see right away the results of our tilling the soil, planting seeds, and watering, things are actually changing very rapidly. So it is with our lives, and our practice of Buddhism. The changes are occurring though it may take time for those changes to manifest.

Think of your practice in this way, you are eliminating the ruts in your life. You are changing the patterns of behavior that have accumulated over lifetimes.

Continue today to observe your Right Ways as well as your connections. Consider these practices as ways in which you are nourishing the causes to your enlightenment.

DAY 31

Read Lotus Sutra
M p. 308 beginning of Chapter XXIV
"Thereupon Sakyamuni Buddha
faced east...(continue to p.
309)...Do not consider that that
world is inferior to our!"
R p. 363 beginning of Chapter XXIV
"At that time Shakyamuni Buddha
entered...(continue to p. 364)...it
bodhisattvas, or the land there."

Wonderful-Voice bodhisattva

After you have completed today's
reading, split your remaining time between chanting Namu
Myoho Renge Kyo and reciting the Shindoku of Chapter 16. If
you are able to complete your reciting of Chapter 16 in less
time, then spend the extra time chanting Namu Myoho Renge
Kyo. But remember there is no rush to complete reciting
Chapter 16.

In all aspects of our Buddhist practice we should not rush. As I
mentioned when we first began I am reluctant to place time
limits or restrictions on our practice. However, for the purpose
of this introductory practice time gives us some structure.
Eventually I hope you shift to a practice that is based upon
your personal needs.

We are nearing the end of the 35 days and as we approach this
point it would be my wish that you be mindful of what you are

feeling as you practice. Eventually as you become more proficient in chanting the Shindoku of Chapter 16 you can spend more of your time chanting Namu Myoho Renge Kyo. As that occurs hopefully you will transition to chanting not for time but for fulfillment, or until you are full.

The portion we read today in the Lotus Sutra talks about a practitioner of the Lotus Sutra in another world that has been illuminated by the Buddha of our world, Shakyamuni. I would like for you to think about the passage where the Buddha of that other world instructs Wonderful-Voice Bodhisattva not to disparage this world in which we live, this Saha World.

Wonderful-Voice is told not to think less of this world, our world, just because it is full of mud, stones, and impurities. I think this is an important reminder for us. We should not think that we are somehow inferior, or that our faults are something to be ashamed of.

There is much in society that seeks to have us believe that we are somehow inferior. Think about advertisements for example, the whole purpose of advertisements is to convince you that you are incomplete, or lacking, or inferior to some ideal because you don't use a particular product. You may have even received messages in school or growing up, which you carry around, that make you feel you are not worthy of being happy.

The message of this chapter is that there is not one among us who is disqualified from attaining enlightenment or of being happy. We are not missing anything, nor are we short of anything, nor are we not good enough to become Buddhas.

Think back to yesterday and I mentioned about the torch dispelling darkness from a cave regardless of the time the cave had been dark. Our lives are in darkness before we begin to practice Buddhism. We are in fact wandering around trying to become happy, yet frequently we stumble or we make wrong efforts. The Lotus Sutra illuminates our life, and our Buddhist practice allows us to see how to live in such a way as to cease our sufferings.

The life you are is perfect for becoming a Buddha like no other. You have unique qualities and talents and are perfectly suited to become enlightened. You do not need to become someone else, you merely need to become your true self. So do not think less of yourself, we all have faults and shortcomings but we can polish those rough spots up and revel the true gem of our lives.

Please continue with your practice of mindfulness, of your connections to other living beings, as well as your efforts observing the Right Ways you have selected to work on.

DAY 32

Read Lotus Sutra
M p. 319 "Endless-Intent! This World-Voice-Perceiver
Bodhisattva does...(continue to p. 320)...the other to the stupa of
Many-Treasures Buddha."
R p. 375 "Inexhaustible Mind, such are the blessings...(continue
to on same page)...the other to the stupa of Abundant Treasures
Buddha."

World-Voice-Perceiver Bodhisattva or Avalokitesvara Bodhisattva
Kannon or Kanzeon or Guanyin

As in days past please split the remainder of your practice time
between reciting Chapter 16 in Shindoku and chanting Namu
Myoho Renge Kyo.

It would seem that World-Voice-Perceiver has a lot of different
names, fortunately it matters not which one you use. For the
purpose of this writing I will use Kanzeon, which is the
pronunciation of this Bodhisattva's name in the liturgical
Shindoku.

While there is much to read in this chapter, and I hope that you
will go back and read it at some point, I chose this section
because it clearly demonstrates the relationship of this
Bodhisattva to the Lotus Sutra. Something that sometimes is
ignored or forgotten.

The importance of this Bodhisattva, especially in East Asia and
now in the West, more so than other Buddhist cultures, is
widespread and for some is the single focus of their practice or

belief in Buddhism. There are some historical reasons for this and we can see, especially in Chinese Buddhist history, as manifest in archeological discoveries in the cave systems lining the Silk Road, that there began to emerge a distinct and separate worship of Kanzeon around the 6th to 8th century CE.

Prior to the veneration of this Bodhisattva outside the context of the Lotus Sutra, the focus of Lotus Sutra practice and worship, as displayed in paintings and sculpture, was the veneration of the Two Buddhas and their stupa. Soon however, the veneration of Kanzeon became more popular even to the point of its association and relation to the Lotus Sutra being ignored or forgotten or discounted. Now, I suspect, there are few average Western believers in Kanzeon who are aware of the relationship to the Lotus Sutra.

As we can see, in this portion we read today, Bodhisattva Kanzeon makes offering to the two Buddhas, Shakyamuni and Many Treasures. This offering demonstrates the subordinate relationship of Kanzeon to these two Buddhas. I think it is also important to notice that the offering of the necklace to Kanzeon was not conditioned upon Kanzeon doing something but for having done something. To me this is an important distinction.

When we approach Kanzeon strictly from the perspective of supplicant to benefactor then we sublimate our own capabilities and our own connection directly to The Eternal Buddha Shakyamuni. This is easy to do if we take Kanzeon out of the context of the Lotus Sutra.

Notice that Kanzeon looks to the Buddhas for permission to receive the necklace and then Buddha instructs Kanzeon to receive the necklace. Once the necklace is received immediately Kanzeon splits the offering and gives it to the Two Buddhas. This clearly demonstrates that Kanzeon is directly tied to the two Buddhas, Many Treasures and Shakyamuni, as their disciple.

The benefits of Kanzeon, and reverence to this Bodhisattva, are directly related to the practice of the Lotus Sutra, and do not replace this Sutra. Our single practice of chanting Namu Myoho Renge Kyo naturally accrue to us all the benefits contained in the Lotus Sutra including those promised by Kanzeon, World Voice Perceiver.

Another thing I would like you to consider is our own function as Bodhisattvas in hearing the cries of others who are suffering. I think that from a perspective of a practitioner of the Lotus Sutra in the age after the death of the Buddha, and given our vows to save all living beings, we actually should be holding Kanzeon as a model for our own behaviors.

It is appropriate to realize that through our many manifestations as original disciples of the Buddha we are in fact representing the many manifestations of Kanzeon. Also, through our vow to spread the Lotus Sutra in this age after the death of the Buddha, and our vow to protect the sutra and its practitioners we naturally fulfill the function of "This World-Voice-Perceiver Bodhisattva does these meritorious deeds. He takes various shapes, walks about many worlds, and saves the living beings of those worlds."

I believe that rather than Kanzeon being a Bodhisattva we rely upon for some benefit, it would be more appropriate to look to Kanzeon as an example of how to live in this age, in this world of suffering. Also our fundamental relationship is directly to and with the Eternal Buddha as original disciples and it isn't necessary to have any intermediary in that relationship.

I hope that you are continuing to work on observing your Right Ways. This is an infinite practice as I am sure you may have realized. There is always something we can improve upon. Buddhism is a quest, an eternal quest for improving our lives, for deepening our enlightenment. Enlightenment is not a terminus, it is not a destination, it is rather a journey; there is no there there.

DAY 33

Read Lotus Sutra
M p. 325 from beginning of Chapter Dharanis "Thereupon Medicine-King Bodhisattva rose...(continue on same page to)...Then he uttered spells:"
M p. 329 "Excellent, excellent! Your merits...(continue to end of chapter)...obtained the truth of birthlessness."
R p. 381 from beginning of Chapter Incantations "At that time Medicine King...(continue on same page to)...Then he made the following incantation."
R p. "The Buddha said to the ogress:...(continue to end of chapter)...accepted the non-arising of all things."

Dharanis/Incantations

After you have finished with today's reading selection please spend the remainder of your practice time divided between reading the Shindoku of Chapter 16 and chanting Namu Myoho Renge Kyo. As you are chanting perhaps you might consider these two paragraphs and the merits they discuss that accrue to someone who practices the Lotus Sutra. Also consider the benefit to those who merely praise the Lotus Sutra.

For some people who are practicing, they may be the only or main person in their household who is practicing. There may be a partner or a spouse or sibling or parent who does not practice. I would like for you to take a moment here and see if you can cause a great sense of appreciation to those other people who may not practice, but upon whom you have a deep relationship with. Let the feeling of appreciation include their either direct, or indirect support of you which enables you to practice.

I have frequently spoken with people who are the only practitioner in their household and sometimes they express concern that the other person doesn't practice. To this I have to say, yes they do! By their indirect support of you as a person, and especially if they do not interfere with your belief in and practice of the Lotus Sutra, they are in fact indirectly having a deep relationship with the Lotus Sutra through your practice.

So, from this perspective their relationship with the Lotus Sutra deepens and grows as a direct consequence of your own deepening practice and relationship with the Lotus Sutra. It doesn't make us better, it makes it more important for their happiness to ensure that we do our personal best to uphold and follow as closely as possible the teachings of the Buddha. Through you, they practice!

For those who live alone, you are not off the hook. Your very existence, as we have been working on throughout this series, is dependent upon countless other people so you should practice with appreciation to those people. It is almost as if when you chant or read, or any way in which we carry out the Lotus Sutra, if you can do so with a deep sense of appreciation to all the things that make it possible to do this practice then you are, in a sense, bestowing the Dharma on these people through your humble efforts.

In this chapter there is a series of speakers who provide special prayers or incantations to protect those who practice the Lotus

Sutra. Basically this means that without our personal practice and relationship to the Lotus Sutra, these offerings have no value, it is us who makes them powerful. Yesterday we read about World-Voice-Perceiver, Kanzeon. It is fundamentally the same in that case as well; our practice, our relationship with the Lotus Sutra determines the value of their promises and vows.

We can manifest all of the wonderful and splendid things contained in the Lotus Sutra only through our practice. I am often struck by those who would seek out select persons, Buddha emanations, Bodhisattvas, deities, and such, without connecting them to the teaching in which they belong. The promises and benefits, as has been stated numerous times, are directly related to our practice of the Lotus Sutra; which in this age amounts to chanting Namu Myoho Renge Kyo.

Because the Lotus Sutra represents a collection of all the Buddha's teachings and is understood to reveal the mind and heart and vow of the Buddha it is questionable when people think they can somehow selectively ignore portions of this complete teaching. It fundamentally, I believe represents a mind of arrogance; thinking that perhaps we know more than the Buddha, or that he taught superfluous things.

So, you are probably wondering, if you have read further in this chapter, what some of those weird words mean. Let me say that these strange words are traditionally not translated within the text of the Lotus Sutra. By that I mean they appear as phonetic representations of the original Sanskrit. This isn't to say they have no meaning or are untranslatable.

The prayers fall into several groups. One group is those that are for the health and safety of the practitioner. Another group is those that cover the practitioner's ability to spread the Lotus Sutra. There is one group that deals with wealth saying such things as no one is wealthier than a practitioner of the Dharma, or that there is no wealth greater than the Dharma. Another collection speaks to the compassion of the Buddha, which will benefit believers.

In all cases though these blessings are directly related to practice of the Lotus Sutra.

Finally as you continue throughout your day try to strengthen your efforts to live according to the Eight Right Ways. Also as you go through your day see if you can consider how you can live your life more effectively for the benefit of other living beings. Think of the ways in which you can either directly or indirectly cause other beings to rejoice.

DAY 34

Read Lotus Sutra
M p. 330 from beginning of Chapter "Thereupon the Buddha said...(continue to p. 332)...practice the Way under that Buddha!"
R p. 387 from beginning of Chapter " At that time the Buddha...(continue to p. 389)...pursue the Way under the Buddha."

Two Sons – Pure Treasury and Pure Eyes

Keeping up the rhythm of your practice routine, once you have finished reading the selection today spend the remainder of your practice time divided between reading the Shindoku of Chapter 16 and chanting Namu Myoho Renge Kyo. I haven't mentioned it in a few days, however, I hope you have not forgotten to try to chant Namu Myoho Renge Kyo or hold it in your mind as you go through your daily activities.

Today we read about two sons who because of the supernatural powers they acquired through their Buddhist practice were able convert their father to Buddhism.

Yesterday as we read the chapter on Dharanis or Incantations I wrote about our practice benefiting our friends and family. In other writings I have talked about the difficulty of converting friends and relatives to Buddhism because they know us in ways that others do not. Our close friends and family know all of our faults, so they are not easily convinced of the benefit of our practice until we make some really fundamental and deep changes in our lives.

Our first step in many instances is to merely hold those people in our hearts and sincerely wish they somehow benefit from our practice.

The thing I would like to you to take away from the reading today is the concept of relationship. Throughout this 35-days I have asked you to consider the many ways you are connected to countless other lives. I have asked you to delve deep into these connections so that you can see how their efforts have impacted you, either directly or indirectly.

Today, and a little bit yesterday, I would like for you to consider how you can benefit those countless other living beings you are connected to. If we are not aware of our connection to others, then it would not be possible for us to consider how our practice can benefit them. Just because you do not know the names of the people who laid the asphalt or who pumped the oil out of the ground or who piloted the ship or conveyance for your product to reach you, does not mean that you are not connected to them.

Likewise, just because they do not know you directly doesn't mean they don't receive benefit from your practice.

Sometimes I am asked about vegetarianism. I personally do not feel it is as important to observe vegetarian eating practices, as it is to observe our relationship to the many things that make it possible for us to eat. Even if we practice vegetarian eating habits, we are still connected to those who may not. So our ability to be vegetarian has to include appreciation to those who are not.

I say this because, our practice of Buddhism is made possible because of what we receive from countless others who probably are not Buddhist. When we can live with a great feeling of appreciation to others and not from a feeling of superiority, then we can most effectively cause people to benefit from our humble efforts.

To be able to engage in this kind of mindful practice is, I believe tantamount to performing all of the magical and spectacular tricks the two sons do to convince their father of the benefit of Buddhism. Further, when we receive benefit ourselves if we can have a sense of both appreciation and gratitude, realizing that we ourselves did nothing on our own, we are better able to repay our debt of gratitude.

Throughout the day please continue to observe the Eight Right Ways, as well as your connections to others. Also remember to remind yourself to engage in chanting Namu Myoho Renge Kyo as you go through your day.

DAY 35

Read Lotus Sutra
M p. 336 "World-Honored One! I heard...(continue to p. 337)...if they do these four things."
M p. 339 "Universal-Sage! Anyone who...(continue to p. 340)...and practice just as you do."
R p. 393 "Arriving at Holy Eagle Peak...(continue to p. 394)...certain to acquire this sutra."
R p. 396 "Then Shakyamuni Buddha praised him...(continue to p. 397)...do the work of Universal Sage Bodhisattva."

Four Causes for Personal Appearance of Lotus Sutra

Well today is our last day together in this project. After you have finished your reading for the day spend the remainder of your time reading the Shindoku of Chapter 16 and chanting Namu Myoho Renge Kyo.

I do not know about you, but I am feeling a certain sadness today with the conclusion of this 35 days we have spent together reading and practicing and talking about the Lotus Sutra. I would say there is some definite grief at work here.

As I think about you completing this introductory practice, or for those who have practiced for a long time your refreshing of your practice, I can not help but be hopeful that somehow you will continue to deepen your practice and faith in the wonderful Dharma that is given to us by the Buddha in the Lotus Sutra.

I feel we have been through a lot together. I wish I could speak to you now personally to congratulate you on such a remarkable achievement. I hope you feel a personal sense of accomplishment.

We have read of how hard it will be to practice the Lotus Sutra, and here you have engaged in 35 days of practice and study. We have also read of the great benefits that will manifest in our lives as a result of our efforts in this most difficult of Buddhist practices.

Perhaps for some of you there has been a dramatic change in the way you view your life and your relationship to your environment. For others perhaps it may not have been dramatic, but it was a new way of approaching how you engage your self with others. There will be as many different experiences are there are individuals who practice.

We have now read through some of the portions of the Lotus Sutra I feel are important to be exposed to. We have certainly not read all of the Lotus Sutra, but I don't need to tell you that. I hope that you will use this 35 days as an introduction to your further exploration of the profound teachings contained in this greatest of the Buddhas teachings. At least now, it may not be as confusing or off-putting or complex. I do think you have a basic foundation from which you can launch into an ever-deepening relationship to the Lotus Sutra.

Also you have practiced reading the Shindoku of Chapter 16 so you are perhaps able to join in when you practice with others in community. And you have become accustomed to chanting Namu Myoho Renge Kyo, which may have been strange to you initially.

Today we read of the four things that will cause the great Dharma of the Lotus Sutra to be obtained in our lives. The first is to have faith, and to have no fear of the truth of the Lotus Sutra. Sometimes fear, also expressed as perhaps feeling weird or uncomfortable, can prevent us from achieving our greatest accomplishments.

As you have chanted Namu Myoho Renge Kyo hopefully you have begun to challenge your fear. Perhaps you still harbor a fear of success, as if you may think you would be the sole person who would not benefit or attain enlightenment as a result of this practice. I can assure you, that you along with all other people are equally qualified to become a Buddha, as you are. Sometimes though our fear may stand in the way.

The second thing is to always observe the Six Perfections which include giving generously to support the Dharma, discipline to practice correctly, patience which includes graciousness to both yourself and others, meditation including meditation by chanting and contemplating the Lotus Sutra, and wisdom by manifesting the wisdom residing deep in our lives, the wisdom of the Buddha which we bring out through our chanting Namu Myoho Renge Kyo.

The third thing that will cause the Lotus Sutra to appear to us is to have firm faith. Firm faith means that we see beyond our successes or failures to the depths of our lives and recognize our inherent Buddha potential. It is difficult to practice this Lotus Sutra way, as we have already read. There will be times when things arise that serve to prevent us from practicing. There will also be times when we may feel so good or so much joy that we think we no longer need to practice. Developing firm faith will enable us to see through these illusions and realize that only by continuing unrelentingly in our practice will we be able to absolutely overcome suffering at its most deepest fundamental level.

The fourth thing is to always hold in our heart the vow to save all living beings. When we become sidetracked with our own problems, or with our own gains, to the exclusion of the sufferings of other beings we can no longer experience a relationship with the ultimate teaching of the Buddha contained in the depths of the Lotus Sutra.

In closing let me say that I wish we could spend more time together. I hope that you will connect with a suitable teacher so that you can further deepen your connection to other practitioners of the Lotus Sutra. I also look forward to walking the Way with you as a fellow Bodhisattva from Underground!

My sincerest best wishes for your happiness and the happiness of all those in your life.

With a deep bow and Gassho,

Ryusho 龍昇 Jeffus

APPENDIX
Shindoku in Romanji of portion of Chapter 16

Chapter 16 - Life Span Chapter - Verse section
妙法蓮華経。如来寿量品。第十六

Myo ho ren ge kyo,
nyo rai ju ryo hon,
dai ju roku.
ji ga toku butsu rai,
sho kyo sho ko shu,
mu ryo hyaku sen man,
oku sai a so gi,
jo sep po kyo ke,
mu shu oku shu jo,
ryo nyu o butsu do,
ni rai mu ryo ko,
i do shu jo ko,
ho ben gen ne han,
ni jitsu fu metsu do,
jo ju shi sep po,
ga jo ju o shi,
i sho jin zu riki,
ryo ten do shu jo,
sui gon ni fu ken,
shu ken ga metsu do,
ko ku yo sha ri,
gen kai e ren bo,
ni sho katsu go shin,
shu jo ki shin buku,
shichi jiki i nyu nan,
is shin yoku ken butsu,
fu ji shaku shin myo,
ji ga gyu shu so,
ku shutsu ryo ju sen,
ga ji go shu jo,
jo zai shi fu metsu,

i ho ben riki ko,
gen u metsu fu metsu,
yo koku u shu jo,
ku gyo shin gyo sha,
ga bu o hi chu,
i setsu mu jo ho,
nyo to fu mon shi,
tan ni ga metsu do,
ga ken sho shu jo,
motsu zai o ku kai,
ko fu i gen shin,
ryo go sho katsu go,
in go shin ren bo,
nai shutsu i sep po,
jin zu riki nyo ze,
o a so gi ko,
jo zai ryo ju sen,
gyu yo sho ju sho,
shu jo ken ko jin,
dai ka sho sho ji,
ga shi do an non,
ten nin jo ju man,
on rin sho do kaku,
shu ju ho sho gon,
ho ju ta ke ka,
shu jo sho yu raku,
sho ten kyaku ten ku,
jo sa shu gi gaku,
u man da ra ke,
san butsu gyu dai shu,
ga jo do fu ki,
ni shu ken sho jin,
u fu sho ku no,
nyo ze shitsu ju man,
ze sho zai shu jo,
i aku go in nen,
ka a so gi ko,
fu mon san bo myo,
sho u shu ku doku,

nyu wa shichi jiki sha,
sok kai ken ga shin,
zai shi ni sep po,
waku ji i shi shu,
etsu butsu ju mu ryo,
ku nai ken bus sha,
i setsu butsu nan chi,
ga chi riki nyo ze,
e ko sho mu ryo,
ju myo mu shu ko,
ku shu go sho toku,
nyo to u chi sha,
mot to shi sho gi,
to dan ryo yo jin,
butsu go jip pu ko,
nyo i ze ho ben,
i ji o shi ko,
jitsu zai ni gon shi,
mu no sek ko mo,
ga yaku i se bu,
ku sho ku gen sha,
i bon bu ten do,
jitsu zai ni gon metsu,
i jo ken ga ko,
ni sho kyo shi shin,
ho itsu jaku go yoku,
da o aku do chu,
ga jo chi shu jo,
gyo do fu gyo do,
zui o sho ka do,
i ses shu ju ho,
mai ji sa ze nen,
i ga ryo shu jo,
toku nyu mu jo do,
soku jo ju bus shin.

Connect with me online:

Twitter: @ryusho @myoshoji

Facebook: https://www.facebook.com/Ryusho

Blog: www.myoshoji.org/blog

Made in United States
Troutdale, OR
03/21/2024

18608251R00080